Film in *Society*

Film in *Society*

Edited by
Arthur Asa Berger

Transaction Books
New Brunswick (U.S.A.) and London (U.K.)

Library of Congress Catalog Number: 77-55943
ISBN: 0-87855-245-6 (cloth)
Printed in the United States of America

Library of Congress Cataloging in Publication Data

Main entry under title:

Film in Society.
    Consists of reviews originally published in Society magazine.
    Bibliography: p.
    I. Moving-pictures—Reviews.   I. Berger,
Arthur Asa, 1933-   II. Society.
PN1995.F459   791.43'7   77-55943
ISBN 0-87855-245-6

Contents

Introduction

Society on Film, Film in *Society*

Dimensions of Film

Although *Society* magazine has primarily been interested in social and political questions and their policy implications during the past fifteen years, there has also been a continual concern with culture in its pages and a concerted effort has been made in recent years to include reviews and essays on film. These reviews are written from a wide variety of points of view and you will find, in this book, work by psychiatrists, sociologists, political scientists and literary scholars, to name just a few of the disciplines represented.

As you might expect, the reviews all have a societal focus and are concerned (to a great degree but not exclusively) with what the various films reveal or reflect about the societies in which they were produced. The authors take their films seriously and bring to the films a wide-ranging erudition and sophistication. They are also aware that film is an art form and treat the pictures they deal with as more than documents to be exploited only for their sociological or ideological content.

In an editorial by Paul Willemen in the Spring/Summer 1973 issue of *Screen* on Cinema Semiotics and the Work of Christian Metz we find an attack on traditional ways of dealing with film:

> The most important feature of Christian Metz's work is that it establishes a break in the history of ideas relating to the object film. Up to the time of Metz's intervention (about 1964), film/cinema had been used as an excuse to talk about something else, usually the moral views, the political beliefs and other prejudices of the critic himself. As film had never been regarded as a text, i.e., as the question of pertinence had never been asked with regard to the cinematic discourse, individual critics assumed that no knowledge was required other than the "general culture" of the "well-educated" gentleman/woman. Attempts to change this situation had been in terms of efforts to turn cinema into what it is not (yet): source material for the literary critic, sociologist, psychologist, historian, economist, moral philosopher.

The answer Willemen gives to the question of what one should do with film is to focus on the problem of meaning. "Semiology," he writes, "as the theory of the production of meaning in texts, will have to provide the theoretical framework for any examination/description of film texts; and as linguistics is at present the most advanced branch . . . of semiology, the film semiologist will have to lean heavily on those aspects of the conceptual apparatus of that discipline. . . ."

I think that Willemen raises an important issue. We err when we regard films as *nothing but* source material for critics and sociologists. But we should not neglect the social and political aspects of films in our concern with "meaning." Works of art do not exist in a void and meaning is not something produced out of nothing. One of the problems with much contemporary writing on film is that it is terribly technical and abstruse. And narrow. In their passion for searching out meaning, many semiologists neglect much that is important, such as the fact that films do have social and political dimensions.

The reviews in *Film in Society* recognize the aesthetic as well as the social dimensions of film and do not neglect such matters as performance, editing and stylistic concerns in general. Throughout these reviews you will find dicussions of images, techniques employed by directors to create effects, symbolism, genre analysis as well as such topics as socialization, technology, racism and sexuality.

What I've been trying to suggest here is that this is a real *film* book, full of the concerns of film students and scholars, and it is not a book about society that dips into films only to make points.

On the other hand, this book does what many film books do not do—namely, it focuses upon the relationship between film and society and does not make the mistake of talking about film as if it existed outside of society. Hollywood may be a *dream factory,* as Hortense Powdermaker put it, but its dreams—like all dreams—are rooted in experience. Now that we recognize the significance of collective (or mass-mediated) dreams and daydreams, Hollywood's capacity to generate and conventionalize the expression of these fantasies makes its work all the more important. It may be difficult to work with art forms such as films, which are collaborative efforts and are very complex, but it is worth the effort. We can learn a great deal from our entertainments and arts once we realize they have something to teach us and learn how to go about analyzing them.

As a matter of fact, sometimes studying dreams, visions and collective fantasies such as films is an important way of gaining sociological knowledge. In a fascinating book, *Psychoanalysis and Social Research,* psychiatrist Herbert Hendin points out that frequently individuals are "not consciously aware of most of the significant attitudes and dynamic patterns shaping their thinking and behavior." When asked for information by sociologists, people often give answers they think are expected of them or which they think the interviewer wants to hear. Or they have other defenses which prevent them from giving true answers to opinion surveys.

Hendin mentions some research he conducted in Norway as an example of this. A sociologist has been to Norway and accepted as true statements made to him by women there "that in their country the woman plays a completely submissive role in marriage." What Hendin found when he got the women to discuss their dreams and talk freely was that they perceived themselves as stronger than their husbands, that their mothers had dominated their fathers, etc. These Norwegian women dreamed of their husbands as babies and children. When asked to explain the difference between their dreams and statements to sociologists, the women said "women are stronger than men, but a man must be allowed to think he is stronger."

The expressive arts, such as film, often reflect these unconscious beliefs with stunning accuracy, which may account for the increasing interest and attention that social scientists and other scholars have been paying film (and the various forms of popular culture, in general). Film, which was previously viewed as trivial entertainment, is now looked upon as a remarkable medium of great power and complexity.

Studying Film in *Film in Society*

Film is a medium which transmits many different popular art forms or genres. This fact has determined the organization of this book. If the main focus here is on the relationship that exists between film and society (and aesthetic/stylistic matters relating to the ways in which films communicate), the second focus is upon the various film genres, many of which, themselves, have important social implications. Fortunately, most of the important genres found in film have been reviewed in *Society's* pages, so you will find, here, reviews of horror films, comedies, disaster films, adventure stories, gangster films, detective films, documentaries and neo-documentaries and pornographic "flicks."

Furthermore, the work of many of our most imaginative and significant directors is discussed. The directors covered are giants such as Buñuel, Fellini, Kubrick, Altman, Polanski, Bogdanovich, Wiseman, Coppola and Wertmuller. To add frosting to the cake, the reviews in *Film in Society* deal with many classic films such as *The Graduate, Bonnie and Clyde, THX1138, The Discreet Charm of the Bourgeoisie, Amarcord, Nashville, The Godfather,* and so on.

Thus there is excellent coverage of film as far as genres, directors (or auteurs, if you wish to be fancy), and important films are concerned. Some classically significant stills from many of these pictures have been used, also, to refresh your memories and to serve as points for discussion.

But how does one *intelligently* discuss film?

Modes of Analysis

In this section I deal with a number of different considerations relative to the matter of how one criticizes (which doesn't mean to be negative about) film. Much writing on film is difficult. For example:

> What happens in *systemic* terms is this: the absent-one of shot one is an element of the code that is attracted into the message by means of shot two. When shot two replaces shot one, the absent-one is transferred from the level of enunciation to the level of fiction. As a result of this, the code effectively disappears and the ideological effect of the film is thereby secured. The code which produces an imaginary, ideological effect, is hidden by the message. Unable to see the workings of the code, the spectator is at its mercy. His imaginary is sealed into the film; the spectator thus absorbs an ideological effect without being aware of it, as in the very different system of classical painting.

This quotation is from an influential article, "The Tutor-Code of Classical Cinema" by Daniel Dayan, which was published in *Film Quarterly* and reprinted in Bill Nichols' important collection *Movies and Methods*. It is, of course, somewhat unfair to take a selection from an essay, but I wanted to show how complex and sophisticated some of the work on film has become.

Indeed, as anyone who has spent any time in film societies or who has read some of the classic texts of film criticism can tell you, film theory has now entered the post-metaphysical stage. Immensely sophisticated and sometimes absolutely opaque studies of film as language, film semiotics, image analysis, and film rhetoric fill the journals and bookstores. I once belonged to a film society and found it a fascinating though bewildering experience, as my colleagues informed one another of their particular interests. One said she was only interested in individual frames. After all, a film is a collection of frames, so the design of the elements in a frame is worthy of considerable attention. Another member told me he saw films as, in essence, nothing but "collections of signs and significations." At times I thought I was a member of a think-tank devoted to systems analysis, though there were also Marxists, Freudians and others who brought me back to reality.

The work of the film metaphysicians is interesting and useful, but not always directly related to our concerns—though it is important we understand all the ways of analyzing film, so I will have something to say about semiology, the current rage in film criticism. On the opposite pole, far from the serious critics of film, we find the cinema journalists, who focus their attention on whether they enjoyed a film, whether the acting was good, the plot was well constructed and that kind of thing. This type of criticism is often entertaining but it tends to be shallow.

What you will read here falls between these two devils: the reviews are serious (but never academic) and often profound, but they are all eminently readable and all have "a larger purpose," namely relating film to social and political events. No matter which film from whatever genre we are dealing with, there are certain techniques of analysis that can be used to explore a film's meaning and significance. The purpose of film criticism, as I see it, is to interpret and to explain a film. The term "criticism" has, unfortunately, negative connotations which I alluded to earlier; many people think a critic is someone who points out what is wrong with something. That is not the case at all. *The purpose of analysis or criticism, as far as I am concerned, is to understand—in the most profound sense of the term—a film and to be able to relate it to the society which it reflects—and sometimes affects.*

I have already indicated the first technique that can be applied to film —the sociological point of view. Here we look at such matters as classes dealt with, social problems focused on, and life styles reflected. Please remember that I am arbitrarily separating aesthetic and stylistic matters from sociological and other points of view here, though in fact, a good reviewer never loses sight of the fact that a film is a work of art. This is a "given." What else remains to be elicited from a film, then? That is what I'm dealing with here.

Some sociological matters of interest dealt with in this book are, for example, the question of total institutions which the films of Wiseman investigate, or the matter of anti-Semitism, which finds its way into the black horror film *Blacula.* The review of the Buñuel film considers the question of bourgeois depravity and the *Barry Lyndon* review, in like manner, focuses upon class structure in Europe. These are just a few of the many sociological topics investigated in this book which, I'd like to suggest here, is not only a film book but might also serve very handily as a sociology text, or text supplement.

Closely related to sociological analysis is what might be called ideological analysis—a concern with political themes and topics found in the film, either overtly, as in a film dealing with fascism, such as *Amarcord,* or in an amplied manner, as in discussions of alienation reflected in films like *Nashville* and *Chinatown.* The review of *Burn* deals explicitly

---

Heroes and Heroines in Film

1. Heroes and heroines are, for our purposes, major figures in dramatic stories, adventures, etc. They are not always good, though generally they are more good than bad.

2. Are heroes and heroines people who somehow "shape" events or are they people who "react" to events?

3. Heroes and heroines offer a number of uses (functions) for viewers: *Transcendence* or gaining new identities, *Reinforcement* or securing old identities, *Satisfaction* of needs people have.

4. There are certain important kinds of heroes and heroines: detectives, spies, athletes, adventurers, cowboys, etc. When new kinds of heroic personalities become popular—as in the case of science fiction heroes and heroines—it generally has some social significance.

5. Within each category of hero or heroine there are always specific ones who are most important: Mike Hammer, James Bond, Superman, Gidget, etc. We must account for the popularity of specific heroes and heroines within a given genre.

6. How do our heroes and heroines relate to one another and to other people? What kinds of relationships do we find and what significance do these relationships have?

7. What do the characters do or not do that is of importance? Why?

8. Heroes and heroines offer *role models* for people. What roles tend to be stressed? What effects do these role models have upon people who "identify" with the heroes and heroines? What roles tend to be neglected?

9. How do heroes and heroines affect styles? What hair styles, fashion styles, speech styles, life styles have been started in recent years by different stars?

10. What demographic matters, such as age, occupation, sex, ethnicity, class, religion, race, region, etc., are important? What groups are over-represented and what groups are under-represented?

---

with Marxist-Leninist thought and the question of whether revolutionary films can be commercially successful; in dealing with these topics, a comparison with *The Last Battle of Algiers* is made, which opens up for us the whole area of film and revolution.

Another technique that is used by film critics is that of psychoanalytic interpretation, in which concepts from Freud and Jung and other psychologists and psychiatrists are used to explicate events and explain personal behavior in films. The review of *Bonnie and Clyde* and *The Graduate* was written by a psychiatrist, and though his focus is upon the social criticism found in these films, we find discussions of the Oedipus Complex, sexuality, and other "psychoanalytic" topics throughout the essay. In like manner, the review of Buñuel's *The Discreet Charm of the Bourgeoisie* concerns itself with rituals, symbolizations and dreams—all important subjects for psychoanalytically inclined critics. Psychoanalytical concepts are found pervading the essays, along with the other techniques mentioned, and for a good reason. Film is an art form that makes great use of images and symbolizations, and psychoanalysis is a form of inquiry which deals with these matters and their significance for our psyches. What I am talking about when I say psychoanalytic techniques involves an application of insights and concepts used in psychoanalysis and psychotherapy to film and other art forms.

Film, like other arts, helps us work through various unconscious conflicts and deal with repression, anxiety and other afflictions. Thus, to write about horror in film and neglect explanations by psychoanalysts (who often link horror to old, repressed childhood fears which seem to be coming true) is to put yourself in a conceptual straightjacket; fortunately, the review of *Blacula* is very sensitive to the relationship between our fears and fantasies and societal anxieties in general.

In addition to the techniques I've already discussed—and many reviews use a variety of different techniques at the same time—there is the historical review, which focuses upon such matters as changes, over the years, in a film genre or the events surrounding the making of particular films. Since history involves change over time, historical critics concern themselves with changes and developments in films and tend to be more descriptive than analytical. Thus the review of *Chinatown* uses the film as the occasion for an excursion into the mystery genre and is concerned with the film in question as well as the devitalization of the genre, which the author suggests has taken place.

Many of the reviews have a historical perspective and it is only logical. A given film is, after all, a representative of a genre as well as an individual creation of a writer and director, actors, cameramen and so on. So it is difficult, at times, to talk about a film without making reference to others like it, or other films by the same director. The historical perspective is important because it provides information that helps us understand what the people involved with the film were trying to do and to gain a sense of context.

When the historical focus is directly on the director of a film we have what is called *auteur* criticism. But auteur criticism, which sees the director as an artist and is concerned with the quality of his imagination, his sensitivity and sensibilities, (as well as his difficulties in financing the film and working with others involved)—this type of criticism seems to include all the techniques discussed to this point. Thus you can psychoanalyze the director, discuss his ideological convictions, examine the institutions of society that he deals with, and write a biography of him, all at the same time. The auteur concept is convenient in that it provides a

---

Literary Considerations Relating to Film

1. What is the *subject* of the film? Or are there several subjects?

2. What important *themes* are dealt with? (Some important themes are the destructiveness of jealousy, the importance of freedom, revenge, etc.)

3. What is the *plot* of the film? That is, what happens in the film? Are there any important subplots?

4. Who are the various *characters* and what importance do they have? What do they symbolize?

5. What is the *setting* and what significance does it have?

6. What *ideas* does the film deal with? Does the film have anything to show to tell us about sex, politics, art, identity, love, power, manners, mores, morals, etc.?

7. How well is the *screenplay* written? Is the dialogue interesting or wooden? Is it fitting? Are the characters properly motivated? Are they three-dimensional or one-dimensional.

8. What *techniques* did the writer of the screenplay use? Do we find satire? Parody? Suspense? Horror? Fantasy? Are "flashbacks" used? Is "stream-of-consciousness" used? Are there any other methods (or tricks) used to create effects?

9. What is the *tone* of the film? How do we recognize this tone and what importance does the tone have?

NOTE: For our particular purposes, here, the important thing to remember is that you must learn how to discuss the various components of the film with reference to their literary and sociopolitical significance. Whether or not you like a given film is not the question—though you should be able to justify your opinions for films you do like. Do not make the common error of thinking that you've analyzed a film when you've merely retold the plot. An analysis is not the same thing as a synopsis.

---

focus which enables one to use all the critical techniques in one's repertoire—as long as they are filtered through or directed upon the director.

There is yet another approach which the film critic can use to analyze a film—a technique (a subject matter and an "activity") I've already alluded to earlier, semiology. The focus in semiological analysis is upon relationships and significations. This technique is actually derived from Marxist and psychoanalytical points of view—it is implicit in both —and is concerned more with form than content, though the two are not, in fact, separable.

We find a concern with the structure of films in a number of reviews. For example, the review of *The Discreet Charm* discusses the fact that the film is organized into eight dining segments, which is not only a brilliant editing tactic but also a means of calling our attention to the role of pedestrian activities in everyone's lives.

In a like manner, the structure of *Nashville* is pointed out as vitally significant and this is then compared to that found in *King Kong*. What we discover from this attention to structure and signification is that form has a message as well as content and we ignore the "design" of a film at our peril. Semiological critics are concerned with the matter of *signifiers* and *signifieds*, two barbarisms from the lexicon of the Swiss linguist, de Saussure. The *signified* is a "concept," the *signifier* is a "sound image," and the combination of the two is called a *sign* by de Saussure. The relationship between *signifier* and *signified* is always arbitrary, de Saussure insisted . . . or unmotivated.

In his *Course in General Linguistics* de Saussure wrote:

> Language is a system of signs that express ideas, and is therefore comparable to a system of writing, the alphabet of deaf-mutes, symbolic rites, polite formulas, military signals, etc. But it is the most important of all these systems.

> *A science that studies the life of signs within society* is conceivable; it would be a part of social psychology and consequently of general psychology. I shall call it *semiology* (from Greek sèmeîon "sign"). Semiology would show what constitutes signs, what laws govern them.

This is one of the fundamental statements of semiology. It suggests we look at films (and many other phenomena) as if they were "systems of signs" *within society*. What de Saussure and other semiologists have done is to provide us with a consciously formulated system and a special vocabulary, which helps us study films as "texts" with more precision than had been possible in the past.

Thus the review of *THX 1138* is concerned with the power of visual images (*signifiers*) to convey meaning (*signifieds*) and mentions the film *2001* in passing. Permit me to make a few remarks about this film which will, I believe, help you understand the semiotic technique a bit better. In *2001* the *subject* is outer-space travel. (I will not get involved with the *theme* too much, which seems to be redemption, though others have different views.) Space travel, then, is the *signified*. Our feeling, when we see the film, that we are actually involved with space travel is created by the use of various *signifiers*: rocket ships, astronauts, evocations of weightlessness such as the floating fountain pen, space-food, computers, portrayals of heavenly bodies and so on.

There is another important concept in semiology that is useful and which can be explained without too much difficulty here. This is the notion that meaning stems from relationships, and one relationship in particular—polar oppositions. As de Saussure writes:

> . . . concepts are purely differential and not defined by their positive content but negatively by their relations with the other terms of the system. Their most precise characteristic is in being what the others are not.

Thus "rich" doesn't mean anything unless there is "poor" and "upstairs" isn't possible unless there is a "downstairs." What this means is that films and other art forms either use oppositions overtly, with cowboys in white and killers in black, or imply them. One way or another we must have oppositions, as well as other kinds of relationships.

Thus, to return to *2001* again, the astronauts gained significance because they were compared, indirectly, to their progenitors, the apes. We find the following oppositions in *2001*: apes and astronauts, primitiveness and super technical, clubs and rocketships.

You may wish to continue the list of oppositions, at your pleasure, or find other systems of oppositions in other films. (It is a fascinating business searching for the secret structure which gives meaning to narratives.)

Let me offer a diagram, which shows where we are relative to this matter of analyzing films.

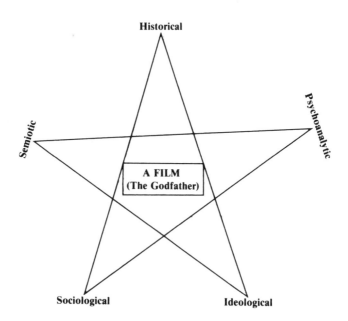

Historical

Psychoanalytic

Semiotic

A FILM
(The Godfather)

Sociological   Ideological

Modes of Film Analysis

The modes of analysis shown in the diagram are only some of the ways that films can be dealt with. What a person *sees* in a film is determined, to a certain extent, by what he or she brings to the film. Perception is frequently *selective* and also, to a certain degree, ideological. And Marxists, Maoists, anarchists, moralists, atheisms, Catholics, scopophiliacs and all kinds of other people representing a wide variety of points of view bring private (and sometimes not-so-private) passions and beliefs to films.

I can't help but think of John Godfrey Saxe's marvelous poem, *The Blind Men and The Elephant*, when I think of the various approaches to film analysis. Each of the blind men touched a different part of the elephant and each then concluded that the elephant was like the part he touched. Let me quote the last stanza of the poem:

And so these men of Indostan
Disputed loud and long
Each in his own opinion
Exceeding stiff and strong,
Though each was partly in the right
And all were in the wrong.

Saxe's warning should be heeded by all critics of film and other art forms. This suggests that we should endeavor to see a film as something situated in society, something which can and should be analyzed from a number of different points of view at the same time.

As I suggested earlier, one of the problems we face in dealing with a film is that it is hard to know *who* is responsible for *what* in the film, since film is a collaborative art form. A successful film is the result of a large number of people who are involved with it being "on form," so to speak.

Film as a Collaborative Enterprise

There is a tendency to give primary responsibility for the creative aspects of a film to the auteur director, who shapes everything, and that is probably correct. However, a great deal depends upon the writer, whose script provides the base on which the film is constructed. Many "bad" scripts are saved by brilliant acting, a good score, great camera work, etc. A film is also the result of a business deal being made, money being lent by banks, stars being signed up (to insure the loans) and a lot of other considerations of a non-aesthetic nature. There are also distributors to be dealt with and, ultimately, the audience. They have to want to see the film and to make the effort to go to a cinema. This matter is more of a problem than it might seem. Statistics indicate that the average

A Check List on Film Criticism

AESTHETIC CRITICISM

1. *How does the film rate aesthetically?* What are its components? What about the performances, lighting, music, script, etc.?

ETHICAL CRITICISM

2. *What moral issues are raised?* Are there any ethical dilemmas dealt with? What is posited as right and wrong?

PSYCHOANALYTIC CRITICISM

3. *What effects does the film have on the psyche?* What needs are dealt with? What gratifications offered? What motivates the characters? Why are we "moved" by the film?

SOCIOLOGICAL CRITICISM

4. *How does the film relate to society?* What do we find in it that involves class, sex, race, ethnicity, stereotypes, etc.? How does the film function in society?

POLITICAL CRITICISM

5. *What is the political/ideological significance of the film?* Do Marxist concepts like alienation, mystification and class conflict explain anything?

SEMIOLOGICAL CRITICISM

6. *How does the film generate meaning?* What signifiers, signifieds, signs and symbols do we find in it? What system of oppositions?

HISTORICAL CRITICISM

7. *How does the film relate to historical experience?* What events does it allude to? How is it related to national character?

MYTH/RITUAL CRITICISM

8. *Are there any mythic or ritualistic aspects of interest?* Relate the story of the film to ancient myths, rites, legends, etc.

ECONOMIC CRITICISM

9. *Are there any economic factors of interest?* What about the cost of production, payment of stars, etc?

THEORETICAL CRITICISM

10. *What about the cinema and society in general?* What theoretical issues of film analysis must be dealt with?

RESEARCH

11. *What have scholars in other disciplines had to say?* Consult journals and books for writings by scholars outside of film per se, as well as film critics.

person over thirty only'sees a few films in a given year. Recent statistics show, for example, that the average American spends 26.4 hours per week watching television and only .06 hours per week attending a movie. (But close to twenty percent of the time spent watching television is devoted to seeing films.) Film attendance is connected to age and the amount of disposable income in one's pockets or pocketbooks, amongst other things.

The following diagram deals with film as a collaborative art form:

Frame/Film and Figure/Ground

Most of us are familiar with the optical illusion that appears below.

The Figure/Ground Illusion

As Herbert Zettl points out in *Sight, Sound, Motion*, "Whenever we assign one graphic element the function of figure, the other part assumes automatically the function of ground." In the figure/ground diagram, we see *either* two profiles *or* a vase, depending upon which element we see as figure and which as ground. I would like to take the figure/ground concept and extend it—so we have a way of dealing with frames in the context of films and films in the context of societies, and so on.

The following chart offers possibilities relative to the matter of frames, films, figures and grounds.

FIGURE	ANALYSIS	GROUND
1. A character X	Descriptive	in a still or frame
2. The character and the rest of the frame	Aesthetic	relative to the film
3. The film	Sociological	and society
4. The film and society	Developmental	and the history of that society
5. The film in its historical context	Comparative	and world history, other societies, etc.
6. The film, its historical context and world history	Mythological	and our character, X.

The Anatomy of an Analysis

This chart shows us what our options are (in terms of what we might wish to focus on) and what kind of analysis is appropriate to any given interest we have. *In this chart, the figure and ground at one level become the figure alone at the next higher level* and the chart "flips" over on itself when the character, X, moves from being a figure at the first level to the ground at the sixth level.

I would like to say something about the kind of analysis that is appropriate at each level. At level 1 we are dealing with an image, which, as Ezra Pound pointed out, "presents an intellectual and emotional complex in an instant of time." Thus we are concerned here with the level of material culture reflected in the image, which for our purposes will be a frame in a film.

Images are resonant and contain a great deal of information. We must learn to examine images, not just look at them. There is a "rhetoric" to images, which is another way of saying that they communicate to us through their use of symbols and significations, which we can interpret on the basis of various codes we learn from our society. For example, a man in a tuxedo connotes something like "high class," though we must always envision our figure in his tuxedo against a background, which may modify this meaning. Thus, a man in a tuxedo carrying a plate of food and bending over people seated at a table now signifies "servant" or "waiter" and implies that the people he is serving are "high class."

What I am suggesting is that we all learn to "read" images on the basis of carefully articulated associations we pick up, and these associations and connections are part of larger systematic structures which I (and others) call *codes*. The context or ground in the "figure-ground" relationships enable us to make more precise interpretations since they indicate the codes we are to use. Because a given symbol or signification is arbitrary, we must learn, somehow, what they mean relative to a given context. This will enable us to make the "correct" interpretation. Let me offer another example: heavy breathing. In the gymnasium context it signifies athletic exertion, while in the bedroom context it suggests sexual passion.

In order to read an image, we must pay attention to all that is stated and implied in a given still. We can do this by carefully describing and listing every signifier (or at least the most important ones) in the still—a task which can be monumental but manageable if we don't press *too* hard. "Everything relates," it has been said, but we need not relate everything to everything else.

As we analyze the elements of the still, we must, at the same time, consider the codings we all have which enable us to make the analysis. The meanings we find in symbols and significations are culturally transmitted ones, so we can examine the various rules of interpretation (which I have called codes) that we carry around with us which make it possible for us to find meaning in stills. What do we bring to a frame that makes it possible for us to "see" signs and significations and to interpret them?

In his essay "Towards a Semiotic Inquiry Into the Television Message," Umberto Eco points out that frequently there are differences between the codes of the creators of works of art and the codes of the receivers of the works of art. For example, a director might think he is conveying "love" in a film and numbers of people who see the film will be getting an entirely different message because they interpret the film or aspects of the film through different codes. He writes, "Codes and sub-codes are applied to the message in the light of a general framework of cultural references, which constitutes the receiver's patrimony of knowledge; his ideological, ethical, religious standpoints; his psychological attitudes; his tastes; his value systems; etc." Since messages imply codes, we can use images to get at the codes which, in turn, are pregnant with information, as Eco reminds us. Not only do films tell stories, then, but so do their most important frames once we learn how to "read" them.

Something should be said about the following topics (relative to the frame):

A. *The figures.* What about their facial expressions, poses, body language, dress, hairstyles, relationships, etc?

B. *The background.* Where is the action taking place and what is the significance of this background? Are there buildings to be seen? What do they suggest? Is the scene in "nature"? If so, what kind of nature? Is the scene in an apartment? If so, how is it decorated and what do we learn from the style of the apartment?

C. *The ambience.* How would you describe what might be called the general ambience of the scene (that is, the figures and the background)? What mood does it strive to create and for what purposes?

D. *The design of the frame.* What kind of arrangement of figures and grounds do you find? Is the arrangement formal or informal? What does the arrangement tell us?

E. *The spatiality.* Related to the general design of the frame is the matter of the use of space. Is the frame "busy" (with a number of elements competing for attention) or is it "simple" with just a few elements and a great deal of white or blank space? What does blank space mean?

F. *The symbols and significations.* What significant signs, symbols, icons, representations, etc. are found in the still? What states of consciousness or fantasy do these images stimulate? What information do these significations convey to us? What conscious and unconscious meanings and associations do they bring to mind?

G. *The themes.* What themes are suggested by the stills? I make a distinction between a theme, which is what a film is about, and a plot, which is what happens, what the characters do (not mean).

H. *The moment in time.* A still is a "frozen moment" which is selected because it has meaning and is significant. We must consider where the still fits in the picture and what its importance is in terms of the narrative development of the film.

When we place the frame in the context of the film as a whole,[1] we are at the level of aesthetic criticism and our concerns are with such matters as the quality of the screenplay, the acting, the photography, and so forth. Here the focus is upon the film itself and how successfully it works, which is, actually, a most complicated matter. At the next higher level we are concerned with the social dimensions of the film itself. Here we deal with such matters as ideology, cultural phenomena, psychoanalytic criticism, etc. (There is, quite obviously, a good deal of overlap and it is hard to separate, with any degree of finality, the kinds of analysis that go on at any given level.)

At the next higher level we place the film, seen in its cultural setting, against the ground of American history. I've labelled this "developmental" analysis but is might also be called "historical" or "evolutionary." It is at this level that concerns with "periods" of American history are focused. Thus, if we are concerned with a film representing the 1970s, we see the film in the context (or against the ground) of the 1970s and the 1970s in the general context of American history. Whatever we deal with here can be dealt with at all four levels of analysis in my chart: the frame relative to the film relative to American society at a given point in time relative to the history of American society.

We need not always cover all the bases but it is important that we realize that they are there, in case we are interested. The level at which most of the essays in this collection operate is the third one, where we learn to read "outward" from the frame to society at large.

We move now to the next logical step, placing American culture as figure, in its historical context, against "world history" as the ground. This is a common means of analysis which I've called "comparative," and we have many comparative literature departments which operate at this level. I believe that American film analysis should be comparative since we need a ground to make sense of our "national" figure. Comparative studies help us discern in what ways we are different or unique and in what ways similar to everyone else.

Finally, the chart "turns on itself" so to speak, and we return to our figure/character at level 1. However, at this level, the history of the world (as represented by the elements in the frame not involving the figure) becomes the figure and our character, X, becomes the ground. What happened in history becomes "congealed" in the frame as the figure and our original character turns out to be our new ground. Instead of seeing the vase in our illusion as the figure we see it as the ground, or vice (vase) versa. I have suggested that we do "myth" criticism here in that the behaviors of individuals often have a mythic aspect, but I'm not sure that mythological criticism is the right term. I must admit it takes a rather courageous leap to see the history of the world (and the universe, by extention) as a figure and an individual as a ground, but I think it can and should be done.

What I've suggested here is an *anatomy* for an analysis—a schema which isolates and shows relationships among the various elements that might be considered when we go about the business of interpreting, explicating, evaluating film (or any kind of art work). I do not mean to suggest that we must cover every level of this "Great Chain of Criticism," but we ought to do as much as we can. In the final analysis it is the sensitivity and knowledge of the critic that is all important. It is his background which enables him to make sense of the characters and figures he deals with. The more you know about the history of the world, the better job you can do making sense of a character in a frame of a film.

*   *   *   *

When we go to the movies we sit between a camera and a screen. The images that flash before us are fascinating and at times so absorbing that we forget we are real people living in a real world. As Plato pointed out, to ignore the real world because of shadows on a cave wall is a terrible mistake. In the case of film, however, these illusions are, if we deal with them correctly, means toward a more profound understanding of ourselves and our society.

Note

1. You can, if you wish, put the frame within a scene and the scene within the film.

Hollywood's New Social Criticism
Bonnie and Clyde and The Graduate

Robert Coles

In this country, it is hard for us to know when a "trend" is established, when a fad is on its way (or is over), and when a movie is the first splash of yet another (new, always new) "wave." We are so self-conscious, so analytical, and so able to let one another know what we're doing that we not only generate critical prophesies, but by the same token defy them or undo them by discussing and examining them to death.

So I feel properly silly about referring to a "new social criticism" on the basis of two films, *Bonnie and Clyde* and *The Graduate*—from, of all places, Hollywood, which is part Marlboro Country and part the sugar-refining capital of America.

Still, it is twenty years since Hollywood's Samuel Goldwyn gave us social criticism in *The Best Years of Our Lives*, for which—then—we had to be grateful. William Wyler, the director, hinted at all sorts of things. The banker (played by Fredric March) makes a speech about the heartlessness of bankers. The three veterans have gone off to fight a war; but in peacetime, soldiers, sailors, and men from the Air Force must return to what they were, to the class that is theirs. Victorious America has plenty of problems, but ironically it is the well-to-do, the ostensibly happy (they have everything, everything they want) who seem most adrift, most senseless.

From 1946 to now is both a long way and no distance at all. The movies have certainly changed, but the veterans are still coming home from a war, some hurt much more than Harold Russell, the discharged sailor who lost both hands; and the war is one still fought in the name of American principles, in the name of "freedom," and in defense of "our" system against the onslaught of "theirs." Such being the case, I wonder whether some Congressman might not want to take a look at both *Bonnie and Clyde* and *The Graduate*. Are we fighting in Asia so

19

that our "boys" can come home to have the right, the freedom, to see critical films like these?

If William Wyler had vague or half-concealed misgivings about victory in war as a "solution" to anything but a fight, or about America's commitment to social justice, he has successors in Arthur Penn and Mike Nichols—who do not conceal or disguise their views, critical as they are of the basics of American life. Today Penn and Nichols don't have to use any subterfuge—or so these two films seem to suggest—even when Hollywood is paying the bills. Whether other directors will follow their lead may depend on a lot more than the intrinsic value of *Bonnie and Clyde* and *The Graduate*. What might happen, for instance, if the powerful satire in such films were directed bluntly at our sadly inviting and vulnerable political scene? And what might happen if that political scene degenerates even further; if our leaders feel that silence is necessary, since—after all—we are in the midst of a war that seems endless, awful, and increasingly dangerous?

I suppose "they" in power would be well-advised to start squashing dissent by putting a stop to the appearance of more films like *Bonnie and Clyde* or *The Graduate*. Both of them are grievously un-American; both of them are sly, mocking, disrespectful assaults upon all sorts of things that all of us have been brought up to cherish. Neither of them makes this country seem like the great, near-perfect nation that it is—threatened abroad, but strong, sure of itself, and God-fearing. In fact, the directors of the two films have forsaken the insinuations and implications that a man like William Wyler used to get across so delicately; they have brutally confronted us with both our national history of violence (in the case of *Bonnie and Clyde)* and our foggy moral climate (in the case of *The Graduate)*.

Until *The Graduate* appeared, I thought I would never stop hearing about *Bonnie and Clyde*. My patients told me to see it, and after a while, when I still hadn't, they began to wonder why. Exactly how *old* was I? How square could a guy like me let himself become? Didn't I know that everyone had an idea or two about "the meaning" of the movie? Since my patients are students and teachers, and my present research is now done in a ghetto and in a white lower middle-class neighborhood, I had to notice that no one on the *other* side of town—black or white—had seen or cared to see *Bonnie and Clyde*. Nor was it possible to attribute that fact to the high price of admission to a first-run movie house. Other films—*Cool Hand Luke*, for instance—could draw the interest, if not the attendance, of the youths I know. They knew about that when it first hit town, and they managed to get to see it right away.

In Cambridge, though—and in communities like it all over—*Bonnie and Clyde* has been all the rage, and for good reason. The director, Arthur Penn, clearly had a number of *ideas* on his mind when he made the film, and I think he makes a certain kind of viewer his ally rather quickly. Supposedly we are to see the "story" of Bonnie Parker and Clyde Barrow, two young robbers who stunned and mesmerized the America of the thirties. We do, of course, see them, but who do they actually become in this film—Bonnie and Clyde, and the Barrow "gang," which includes Clyde's brother and sister-in-law, and his new friend C. W. Moss? Rather obviously they become "us"—and I don't mean "us" exactly or "realistically," but us the viewer, the person who reads books and has gone to college and considers himself or herself "imaginative," or "socially responsible"—and, of course, "critical." The "beautiful people," after all, are *part* artistic and theatrical and intellectual, or at least think of themselves as such. They try hard to mix beauty and social class with a scattering of "creative" people. They also scorn "middle-class morality," which teaches us to be chaste, then monogamous, and tight with money, and exceedingly obedient; in T. S. Eliot's words, "cautious, politic, meticulous."

"Smart" Young Critics

Since *Bonnie and Clyde* appeared, much has been made of Warren Beatty and Faye Dunaway, but I think I never realized how broad and limited their "appeal" is until I heard them discussed by some lower middle-class white youths—young factory workers. "Why did you ask us to go see *that?* They're a bunch, all of them. But mostly those two, I mean the girl Bonnie and her friend Clyde. You can't tell me it was like that, the real gang. You know what I think? I think the whole picture, it's like a lot of college kids having a big time for themselves. I mean, it wasn't real, you know. What gets me is that they try to tell you it was based on a true gang, but then you see them, and they're like wise-guy kids having a good time for themselves—and they're so lousy *smart* about everything."

His friend found the movie a "waste of time," though a minute later he added an important qualifier: "The only thing good was the ending." Hungrily I wanted to know why. "I don't know, it was just good," he said. Then suddenly he *did* know: "Maybe because it was true, you could think to yourself that it happened like that. The rest of it, I thought they were just trying to be *smart.* "

Again I had heard that word "smart" used—accurately, I believe. Without college degrees, with no interest in symbolism or cinematography or social protest or a subject like "violence in American life," they had spotted the alien and the enemy. And if one forgets the

In the 1930s and 1940s the men whom Robinson, Cagney, and Bogart portrayed came close to us. They were mobsters or antisocial and only reluctantly on the "right" side. But America itself was in an awful mess . . . .

pejorative implications of the word "smart," they had also spotted the very thing Arthur Penn and Warren Beatty had in mind to do—be very smart about all sorts of things that went on and are still going on in America.

Bonnie and Clyde makes a decisive break with the past, with films that have starred Edward G. Robinson, James Cagney, and above all Bogart. Until now, men like those three could unite polite, intellectual society and the "ordinary," unself-conscious viewer, be he the factory worker or the "thoughtless" businessman—whom snobbish academics take such pride and satisfaction in having around to scorn. In movie after movie these three gave us gangsters, tragic juvenile delinquents from Hell's Kitchen, or clever cynics who were "above" parties, postures, and positions. They were ugly and insulting and murderous at the drop of a hat, yet again and again they invoked our sympathy—because we were enabled to give it, even encouraged to. It is safe, even morally correct, to love an errant neighbor: No matter how bad, how treacherous, how sour, crabbed, and sullen a person is, he can be "saved," prayed for, offered our hope—and more, because we have all learned that "there but for the grace of God go I."

Particularly in the thirties and forties the men whom Robinson, Cagney, and Bogart portrayed came close to us. They were mobsters or antisocial and only reluctantly on the "right" side. But America itself was in an awful mess, not some vague "spiritual struggle" but a widespread and concrete collapse of the economic system. There were dozens of reasons for the most respectable of people to feel like shaky, impoverished near-outsiders, to sympathize with the gangster. Not that Hollywood ever really cared to look candidly at a social and economic system loaded with injustice. Cagney or Robinson might earn our sly assent or understanding with a remark here, a gesture there; or Bogart might earn much more, a kind of elusive envy that emerges as adulation for someone who can beat the system, say to hell with it, choose his own kind of life, be smooth and cavalier and insulting and foxy and tricky and open-hearted and breezy and gentle and successful with all the dames —even the toughest, classiest ones. It was even possible for them to make some dough—and not get fired for being "wise" or different or (at another level) "unorthodox" or "unconventional" or "rebellious."

Of course, no one in Hollywood ever tried to say that Robinson and Cagney were playing anything but tough guys—born good but gone bad. Nor was Bogart, at his most appealing and romantic, anything but *himself*—and his appearance, his dress, his manner, his voice all conspired beautifully to differentiate the hero of *Casablanca* or the anti-hero of *Petrified Forest* from *everyone,* good or bad, high or low. Nevertheless, under those conditions—especially under those conditions, that is, the limited freedom that a "gangster film" provides—it has to be said that Hollywood was not nearly so feeble, cowardly, and morally neutral or indifferent as some critics charge. Even in *Key Largo*—where good and evil come to their purest, least ambiguous, most ennobling confrontation—the amoral leader of the world's betrayed (hence incorrigibly gullible and fascist-prone) *Lumpen-proletariat* is allowed some startling comments about hypocritical, pious Western democracy, the kind that breeds, elevates, and protects dishonest, pretentious Chamberlains, Daladiers, and—well, take your choice today. We are glad to see Edward G. Robinson killed—like a water rat in a boat—but he has not been totally unattractive. Quite the contrary. No one would accuse him of a "credibility gap," and I rather imagine that Céline would have said yes, yes a thousand times to him—as an alternative to the life that those three veterans in *The Best Years of Our Lives* faced upon their return to America.

The point is that up to now the gangster was Hollywood's safest social critic—in the end he could be done away with and arouse no alarm in any "loyal citizen." He looked different, and acted different, and if he occasionally talked different, talked "radical," he would eventually be put down, or on occasion (in Bogart's case) somehow be reconciled to our side—in which case the intellectual could feel enraged at the commercialism, the mushy sentimentality, that was doing the "best" of Bogart in. Since intellectuals also make compromises and get "done in" (and do one another in), Bogart's necessary reconciliation with society (as in *Casablanca)* could even "help" those who protested "esthetically" against what the films did to him—that is, if one operates on such ancient and pre-psychoanalytic truisms as "misery likes company."

Well, what has *Bonnie and Clyde* done to all that, to a virtual tradition of film? Very simply, the movie more or less follows Nietzsche's argument, rather than either Freud's or Marx's, and suggests that neither money nor therapy will quite do—but action will, action that flouts the decadent will of a corrupt society, action that exposes old and useless and rotting moralities and establishes a new one by its very example, its presence in the eyes of the (hitherto) deceived onlooker.

Now, America is not all that unable to accept Marx—and as for Freud, no comment is needed. Marx and the first John D. Rockefeller shared a high estimate of the power that money provides, the power to change history. Rockefeller's colleague, Henry Ford, may have called history "bunk," but he never doubted for a moment that he had made history—and he knew that his money enabled him to influence it, fight it, and in the clutch yield to it with a surprising, disarming, and edifying gesture, the Ford Foundation. What neither Marx, nor Stalin, nor Kosygin, nor Mao, nor any members of our government can take is a private, personal, attractive, appealing assault on *order*—on social order, be it capitalistic or statist or a fusion of the two. In that sense, *Bonnie and Clyde* is anarchistic and revolutionary, to give those heavily political labels a more philosophical (and Nietzschean) turn; and *The Graduate* is no less "subversive" and even more "dangerous" because it is a contemporary film rather than an evocation of the past, no matter how slyly Arthur Penn has directed it toward continually "relevant" problems.

As everyone has noticed, Bonnie and Clyde, robbers and murderers, are played by a handsome man and a delicious, fair, blooming girl—as we say in the South, a "tough woman," meaning a decidedly beautiful girl who knows it, and consequently has spunk or self-confidence. What do the two of them do? They turn wayward, overlooked, futile, static lives into prominent, envied, defiant lives, into successfully but nonchalantly acquisitive lives—lives that above all are full of speed, movement, daring. In so doing they manage to topple any number of American pieties—political ones, like the doctrine of "states rights" (they race back and forth over state lines and make a mockery of local sovereignty); and contemporary psychological ones, like the notion that sexual hang-ups may be evaded, denied, run away from, but never "solved" or "cured" if serious enough, if *damaging* or *paralyzing,* as I hear my colleagues say with a certain force, a certain conviction that sometimes shades into gusto.

In fact the film is interesting for how seriously it takes the accidental, nonexplanatory view of human development. Again, I suppose the tradition that has to be invoked, for all its cheapened fate, is the existential one, of Nietzsche and also Camus. Bonnie and Clyde meet by accident— he is surveying her family's car and preparing to steal it. Clyde commits a murder almost by accident—and their bank robberies seem almost secondary to the pleasure they stumble upon, the personal and social breakthrough they seem to achieve. After all, Clyde's brother and sister-in-law join them, and C. W. Moss, too. Actually, they don't really join; they happen along, get drawn in. They are—in today's inevitable word—a "group," who squabble but also gain strength and imagination from one another. And—dangerously—they not only look fascinating, but they go on to act like winners and seducers, like livers of charmed lives. They kidnap a stuffy, decorous, prosperous couple, and make them laugh, forget themselves, and seem for the first time "human," amusing, alive —free of the front porch that adorns their middle-class house. They also turn the police—including, be it remembered, a tall, determined Texas Ranger—into particularly grim, oafish, and heartless characters.

They eat, too—no mean achievement in the depression. In the beginning, some stunning camera work provides the scenes that Dorothea Lange and Walker Evans made unforgettable, the bleak farmland that nevertheless suggests an earlier richness. Somehow generations of courage and labor had been betrayed and become mortgaged to the very banks that Bonnie and Clyde robbed—and one bank is shown to have nothing left in it to rob. Among people of the "great" Midwest, the nation's granary, hunger was a commonplace in the thirties; but Bonnie and Clyde get their ample groceries, feel on top of the world, and do not miss how hungrily fascinated with them the public is—on radio, in the newspapers, and in notices that promise increasing amounts of scare money to informants, while any old workingman is lucky to get a W.P.A. job or a bit of the dole.

So, they go; or rather they go, go, go, just as the auto companies say we can if we buy a Mustang or a Camaro or whatever. Before the F.B.I. really got started, Bonnie and Clyde saw the country as one whole, big chunk of land; and before Dwight Eisenhower's federal road plan, they knew that—as one slogan has it—"America is on wheels." In truth, Bonnie and Clyde were supposed to have had a Robin Hood quality. Or was it that in the thirties we desperately needed our Robin Hoods, and like everything else we took them where we found them? And it isn't easy to be stubbornly generous in America. Even President Roosevelt, who appears in the film on a campaign poster, was called a traitor, slightly worse than a robber, for worrying about the wrong kind of people, among whom unquestionably we can count Bonnie and Clyde and the Negro caretaker they prompt to shoot at his boss's lost home.

In the end "law and order" win, though our sympathies are with the "outlaws" all the way, without reservations—in fact shockingly so. "Crime" has made Bonnie more gentle, giving, and relaxed. Through "crime" she found her man. "Crime"—unassisted by "therapy"—made Clyde famous and made him potent; and, for a change in a Hollywood movie, sex is given at least the *hint* of a kind of ambiguity that I fear is lost on both movie directors and on all too many psychiatrists. For a moment "crime" even makes Clyde's dry, pouting sister-in-law seem funny, pleasing, jolly. As for C. W. Moss, he becomes all sorts of things, court jester, agent extraordinaire, handyman, a binding, healing "force"—and the eventual key to the downfall of his heroes. He offers Bonnie and Clyde refuge in his father's home, but his father turns them in and arranges their deaths.

What about that death scene, with its blaze of bullets? Who is to say? The charmed and charming couple, the pair who wanted to prove that life could be more than drab, even exciting, the couple who took pleasure not only in being noticed, in winning out, but in giving to the needy—they are gunned down in an automobile and in an ambush that makes a Texas Ranger the victor. Like everyone else, movie-makers live in history, and I suppose have the same trouble we all have in sorting out what is irrational, what is accidental, and what is purposeful in the politics, the news, and the tragedies of a given age.

Anyway, one thing the film *does* provide is the protection of distance. Bonnie and Clyde have long since been dead, and they can be dismissed as "period" characters. The country has changed, the world has changed, we all have changed—or so we (and director Penn and his actors) can wryly say and not quite believe.

The Scene Today

Mike Nichols has a different problem. Like Penn he is not altogether taken with what is so often called the "quality" of American life, but in *The Graduate* he was making a film that could not both say a lot and draw upon the past and draw upon the past for protection. His subject *is* —it is not concern with the landscape of the thirties, but with today's: the elaborate or modest but proud swimming pools, the sculptured lawns, the drive-ins and the cook-out spaces that cover the land. He wants us to look at what we can see everyday, anyplace, here, at home in America—oh, not anyplace, I suppose (we do have those bothersome ghettos and Appalachia and the rural South and the Indian reservations and the migrant camps and the farms near towns like Delano), but not *only* in Southern California, where in *The Graduate* a young man finds himself at loose ends after four years at an Eastern college.

In ironic contrast to *Bonnie and Clyde*, Mike Nichols casts Dustin Hoffman in the lead role: Warren Beatty and Faye Dunaway make the outsider glamorous; Dustin Hoffman's ordinary, unspectacular looks make us instantly begin to wonder about him, about what goes on inside the well-to-do, well-educated insider. And that is what Mr. Nichols tells us right off we are going to do.

As the credit lines unfold, Ben is on an airplane, coming home to Los Angeles from "the East." We see him first, his plain face, his dress, his still, slightly preoccupied manner, no different from anyone else's in the plane or, later, in the airport. Then he is home, the guest-of-honor at a party his parents have thrown. They all appear, the lawyers and doctors and businessmen who eat well, drink well, swim well, sun themselves well, and in general have it made in America's swinging sixties. We also see Ben. He is surrounded by admirers—that is, people who respect his scholastic achievements—but he is also very much alone. He *feels* lonely. He is sulky. He broods and turns away from people. (The camera follows him closely as he tries to shake off his unwanted audience.) Outside his house stands a red Alfa-Romeo, a graduation present—and he seems closer to that than to anyone or anything. His parents, who live in a city that is loaded with psychiatrists, in an area that exports on celluloid the cheapest kind of psychoanalytic flotsam and jetsam, know enough to ask whether he is *worried.* Eventually he escapes upstairs to his room, unwittingly followed by Mrs. Robinson, the wife of his father's business partner. She wants him. She gets him. The movie takes up what happens afterwards to her and to him and later to her daughter Elaine, whom Ben does not seek out but meets, likes very much, wants to marry, and at the end after much confusion does win—by taking her away after she has been married to a tall, handsome, blond-haired, blue-eyed medical student, a Mr. Clean if there ever was one.

Perhaps the plot is a little unusual; in the imbroglio we have a young man, an older woman, and the woman's daughter. It's all very "oedipal" —Ben and his *father's* partner and *his* wife and *their* daughter—as we post-Freudians take great pride in saying; all of which means very little, really, except that we have taken a man's idea, a concept he once used to describe a particular set of circumstances, and turned it into a cheap word, a slangy short-cut to nowhere. To Mike Nichols' great credit the film does not get sidetracked into yet another analysis of a sexual hang-up, any more than Arthur Penn lets *Bonnie and Clyde* be the millionth Hollywood clinical study of desire and impotence. What Nichols is after has to do with public tone rather than private temperament, or, more exactly, with the way social customs and cultural styles affect the individual's mind (and heart) and particularly so at a moment of crisis, of transition, of growth. (I suppose it could be said that Nichols has read his Erik Erikson; certainly the movie goes back and forth between accurate, if not always merciful, social satire and sharp psychological portrayal. And certainly Ben's particular vulnerability, but also his foothold on redemption, are shrewdly tied to his age, his recent graduation—in Erickson's phrase, so much used and so flagrantly abused today, his "identity crisis.")

At moments the dialogue in *The Graduate* sounds very much like one of those Mike Nichols–Elaine May records—which is fine by me. Except for the Dr. Blauberman, whom Lillian Ross did us the favor of portraying a while back in *Vertical and Horizontal,* the Nichols-May team was alone in catching the silly banalities that Freud's magnificent work has come to—in the hands of a certain breed of American "practitioners" whose intellectual interests are (let us say) shaky, and whose general intelligence, candor, generosity, and even common sense can on occasion be found questionable.

Whether the scene takes place in a living room, a bedroom, or a kitchen, Nichols grimly brings out the nonsense, the drivel that passes for polite and even "civilized" or intimate conversation. Perhaps he is heartless at times; perhaps he does become a victim of his own shrewd, relentless, pitiless glare—in the sense that the cheapness, the vulgarity, the dishonest, pretentious, fake sentimentality that he documents so constantly will naturally be seen by the viewer as his, the director's. *The Graduate* is thus called a shiny, glossy film, clever and amusing but "basically" (the word or words, the judgment of judgments) dishonest—when in fact the whole point of the film is to portray the thinness of a certain kind of rich, sensual world.

Ben's first lover, a fortyish, self-proclaimed "alcoholic" and "neurotic," is actually given an almost elegantly compassionate reading by Nichols and Anne Bancroft. She grows on us slowly, as we begin to sense what is in her, what has happened to her. At the right moment Nichols holds off the conversation, in fact does a brilliant parody of silence—between a man and a woman who do not really make love but go at it night after night, again and again, without the slightest evidence that anything else can possibly happen between them. For all her "cool," Mrs. Robinson finally disintegrates before our eyes. Anne Bancroft is a sure, disciplined actress; she knows how to take a pitiable kind of indignity and give it a dignified (and gently humorous) interpretation.

Ben meets Mrs. Robinson's daughter, Elaine, because his parents know nothing of his affair with the girl's mother and simply want their boy to meet a nice girl, especially one who is the daughter of their friends. Ben, out of loyalty to Elaine's mother, his lover, who forbade him even the one date his parents prompted, tries hard to be cruel to the girl, but fails. They begin to fall in love. Elaine's mother intervenes and threatens to tell "all." Ben does it first—and, predictably, Elaine flees the scene. She returns to school, and Ben follows her.

The movie takes a critical turn now, one that has annoyed a number of critics. To spoof the upper reaches of the California bourgeoisie is one thing, but one cannot then insist that Ben is, after all, real and not a satirist's tool. It is as if Nichols were being told that the dreary mediocrity he etches out cannot be persuaded to let anyone out of its clutches, in real life or in a film. Once tainted, always no good. Some critics go further: Ben from the beginning is self-centered and spoiled and all that. What "right"—the word one reviewer uses—does he have to rebel against society, against the society that, just about every critic agrees,

Nichols successfully ridicules? Once tainted, always obliged to stay no good.

In fact neither Nichols nor anyone else has figured out how youths like Ben and Elaine come about, in view of the ornately shabby, empty world that "nurtures" them, if that is the word. That is the central, haunting question of *The Graduate*—never stated but *there*. After the movie I found myself thinking how similar those two were, Ben and Elaine—struggling, torn, but not by any means dead—to the men and women I have come to know in Mississippi. There, too, for a different set of reasons, and in a different way, people are brutalized, made cheap, humiliated, turned into shells of themselves. Yet somehow in each generation a few—and it seems, under an enabling historical moment, more than a few—emerge with impressive possibilities, potentialities, dignity, whatever. In the early sixties we used to try to "explain" that irony, and never really did very satisfactorily—except to affirm the cliché that there's more going on in people than words like "past" or "environment" or "problems" or "personality" quite encompass.

So a critic is wrong when he says that Ben is not believable because he, who did so well in college and comes from the home we see, cannot be shy and awkward and offbeat and moody; and a critic is wrong when he claims that a woman like Mrs. Robinson would go after only a beautiful specimen, a surf boy rather than Ben; and a critic is wrong when he insists that a wandering, indulged youth cannot suddenly bring himself up short and find a purpose and go tenaciously after that purpose—a person, a place, a thing, a job. Confident children lose their tongues and manners when they come home. Rich, middle-aged women become as desperate as anyone else—and desperately try to shed themselves of the very cursed, glittery comforts and values the years have given them. And finally, redemption is always possible, among the high and the low—and suddenly, as well as after ten years of psychoanalysis.

Nichols does add a touch of heavy symbolism to the end of *The Graduate*—after Elaine runs to him, Ben uses a cross to bolt the church doors and frustrate their pursuers. Yet why can a novelist experiment with mixtures of realism, surrealism, and social satire, but not a playwright or a director? Why do we always ask whether a movie's character is a "real-life" one? Bonnie and Clyde, as given us by Arthur Penn, are not "real," nor are Ben and Elaine. But they bring out all sorts of real things, realities about us and our lives and our society that we all too easily shirk noticing. In literature the tradition of close, refined, and near-exclusive character study is one of many open to the writer. If he moves deeply into social and historical matters he generally has to call upon "types," upon more representative men and women—though great writers like Faulkner and Tolstoy could do both, build a particular person, and place him accurately or revealingly in a certain kind of world. Neither Arthur Penn nor Mike Nichols would expect to be called "great" at this point, but they are trying very, very hard, if not for greatness, then for achievements that illuminate the quality of American life.

Bonnie and Clyde have ironic companions—from across the railroad tracks—in Ben and Elaine. When Ben comes to that grotesque church in Santa Barbara to get Elaine and run off with her, he wants more than a "nice, attractive" girl—and she more than a mere alternative to the medical student. His drive up and down the beautiful (and ugly) length of California, accompanied by folk-rock music—"light" but "deep," too—has had both drive and purpose behind it, even if their exact nature or fulfillment have yet to be realized, perhaps in another film. Ben stands screaming for Elaine, his arms stretched as in the crucifixion. That too has been called a bit of heavy-handed symbolism, although Nichols has denied such an intent, and although I thought I learned as a child that on every single prosaic day we live and die, are saved or condemned—let alone on days when we make a decision to get married and commit ourselves to a loved one.

Ben doesn't lose Elaine; they go off together in a bus, stared at incredulously, she in her wedding dress, he ragged and unshaven. It is a "happy" moment as the camera fades out. For all the world the accompanying music could now be that same light-hearted, confident, jazzy, racy score that carried us along with Bonnie and Clyde. Ben and Elaine will never be hunted down by the police, but things may well get increasingly scary and desperate: Men will continue to die from hunger, and the "restlessness" that Lyndon B. Johnson mentioned but quickly dismissed could linger on and worsen. So, like Bonnie and Clyde, Ben and Elaine will also need their irreverent melodies or droll songs.

Nashville and America in One Dimension

Richard A. Peterson

The movie *Nashville* continues to be a prime topic of conversation among New York writers half a year after its release, according to John Leonard of the *New York Times* news service. Impressive for any movie, what accounts for the staying power of this musical set among the denizens of country music city? One of the fascinations is surely the film's structure. In it a large number of characters act out their parts without ever once interacting. No one character touches another; none learns from experience. Like two-year-olds in a sand box, they only coact. Since the great engine drama in Western society from soap opera to grand opera is character development, the coaction strategy of *Nashville* is singularly arresting.

The coacting strategy is strongly reminiscent of *King Kong*. In that 1933 minor classic it is an artistic device intended to facilitate the action; in the 1975 film coaction has become a representation of how people really are. While both films end with the senseless killing of the most nearly innocent protagonist, the 1933 killing of Kong atop the Empire State Building by wasp-like airplanes is the inevitable finale of a fast-paced set of events which carry the story around the globe from civilization to the primordial jungle and back. The 1975 killing, though presaged by numerous references to political assassination, becomes a cheap dramatic shot when the country music princess and not the populist politician is targeted. Assassinations may be judged to be senseless, but presumably they have meaning for the person pulling the trigger. In this film the cues remain so scrambled, even after three viewings, that the quest for meaning is easily short-circuited by thoughts like those expressed by Nashville record producer Billy Sherrill (creator of the country music ingenue Tanya Tucker): "She sang so bad, she deserved to die."

A second way in which *King Kong* bests *Nashville* is in the number of characters. Since there is no character development, the dramatic development must depend on the mix of actors. In *King Kong* each character plays a classical role: innocence, purity, lust, activism, pride, greed, and the like. While the focus of *King Kong* is a passion play in which good apparently triumphs over evil, each actor in fact contributes to the appearance of rectitude while revealing contemporary society to be far more insincere, brutish, and cruel than the beast who is slain.

Nashville has been widely promoted as interweaving the lives of twenty-four different people, but, in fact, they all act from the same motive: the desire to maintain appearances at all costs. The political advance man, the motorcycle-riding magician, and the BBC reporter are all professional illusionists. The fading male performer continually tries to promote his own fortune by tying his career to the reputation of the Nashville music industry. To the BBC reporter, the black country music artist pretends that he is someone else. For the benefit of the political advance man, the folk-rock couple pretend domestic bliss in the midst of the debris of their titanic quarrel. The manager-husband of the country music princess pretends gratitude to the rival singer for substituting for his sick wife. The Opryland crowd becomes restless and surly when the ailing singer breaks the veil of image and talks about her real youth. When the illusion is forcibly broken, as at Opryland and in the club where a black man accuses the black performer of selling out his race, the response is not confrontation but flight. Appearance is all.

The use of deception to maintain appearances is most striking in the numerous instances of self-deception, of which there are several striking examples in the film. For example, after cutting off the phone conversation with his mother in a childish quarrel, the killer continues to talk into the dead receiver affirming his tender love for Mom. The stripper-would-be-singer continues to believe that she will become a star despite the massive evidence to the contrary. And while the folk-rock Don Juan begins a new liaison, the devoted wife and mother gospel singer whom he has just scored continues to carry on the pretense of her affair with him with kisses and goodbye waves at the door.

While *King Kong* interweaves a number of interesting homogeneous and unself-conscious parts to create a society of indifference and pretense, *Nashville* makes everyone an indifferent pretender. This world view is underscored in the lines of the theme song that is interwoven through the film: "You may say that I ain't free, but it don't worry me."

At the level of the senses, *Nashville* is a stunning success. The multiple-track sound often carries several distinct conversations to the ear, simultaneously building a feeling of creative tension. As in life, one must continually choose which elements to hear and which to block out. In ad-

dition, scenes are intercut in such a way that, although apparently uncon-
nected, they comment and build on each other. Although it has only
scratched the surface of this technique, the movie suggests that it would
be possible to make a film from which many different interpretations can
be drawn depending on which of numerous equally prominent elements
members of the audience choose to see and hear.

However future critics may evaluate the content of the movie, *Nashville* will undoubtedly become a benchmark in the history of film, showing the way from linear plot toward films of mosaic form. In this role it

However future critics may evaluate the content of the movie, Nashville *will undoubtedly become a benchmark in the history of film, showing the way from linear
plot toward films of mosaic form.*

will be compared with the most structurally original book of 1975, *Ragtime.* The film version of *Ragtime,* being filmed by *Nashville* creator Robert Altman, should be most powerful; he will have a strong story already set in mosaic form and a plot awash in what Greil Marcus, writing in the *Village Voice,* identifies as the "failure of America" pathos.

Seeing the movie in Nashville was a special treat. The locations were familiar and many of the backup musicians and crowd-scene participants were recognizable, thus heightening the sense of newsreel reality. Art and life mingled at a number of points during the gala Nashville opening. The huge flag, high school marching band, "Walker talker truck," and WNGE-TV cameras were all there. Pretty little Miss Georgia, Cindy Burns of Dalton, bounded forward to present Ronnee Blakely an armful of roses. Nashville County Sheriff Fate Thomas presented Keith Carradine, who played the drug-taking seducer, the keys to the county jail. And, as if to confirm that the Haven Hamilton lines were patterned after him rather than Hank Snow, Roy Acuff appeared at the opening "just in from a performance in Indiana" and heading for an appearance at the Grand Ole Opry. He stayed just long enough to venture the booster line, "I can see nothing but good coming from it for Nashville and country music."

The local reactions to the movie have been as diverse as they have been predictable. The cultured set thinks that the views of the Grand Ole Opry should be counterbalanced by scenes from the symphony orchestra and plans for the new civic cultural center. The Methodist ladies groups decides that since Nashville is a church town, a movie called *Nashville* should focus on their activities. The two local newspapers, as usual, split on the issue. The Southern tribal *Banner* sees the movie as another instance of decadent, carpetbagging Yankee exploitations, while the knee-jerk cosmopolitan *Tennessean* takes pride in Nashville being recognized as a metaphor for America.

The newspaper quotations of local reaction, as well as those I have collected from country music industry people, fall into two understandable piles. One group criticizes a particular element as false and thus dismisses the film, while the other praises the accuracy of the general presentation. The former reaction comes from persons with a public image to protect, the latter from behind-the-scenes people and less successful performers.

One Opry perennial walked out in the middle of the premier saying, "I've had enough. I'm not going to sit in a chair that long and be slapped in the face." Others left because they were bored. As one industry person told me, "That's what I do all day. I don't need to pay good money to sit and watch it." People taking this view are not accustomed to seeking meaning for their world in movies. As Loretta Lynn, model for the country music princess, said, "I'd probably go see Bambi first." Steel guitarist Lloyd Green (quoted in the Nashville *Banner)* sums up this reaction: "Who wants to go and see one of these complicated 'soap opera' type films, one in which you have to think it all out. We reached the epitome of that when the Watergate hearings were on television. I go to the movies to be entertained, sort of as an escapism, not to be caught up in something." Green echos the movie theme song, "You may say that I ain't free, but it don't worry me." While this song could not really be a country music hit, it is a true anthem of Southern white fatalism.

Jaws and *Nashville,* films of fear and loathing respectively, appeared in the summer of 1975. Each movie made the cover of *Newsweek.* New York critic Judith Christ called the first film "excellent for what it is" and the second "a milestone in creative movie making . . . among the best of American films—an experience on every level." Pauline Kael of the *New Yorker* observed that she watched *Nashville* "in complete happiness," and that the movie shows "the insanity of the fundamentalist culture in which practically the whole population has been turned into groupies." Judith Christ of *New York* magazine wrote that *Nashville* captures America, "a people inured to those outbreaks of violence saturated with the audiovisuals of our time, a drifting, uninvolved nation of benumbed voyeurs," and that it probes "the American malaise" and "should be required viewing before we consider celebration of a Bicentennial." *New York Times* Associate Editor Tom Wicker stated that the movie depicts the "vulgarity, greed, deceit, cruelty, barely contained hysteria, and the frantic lack of root and grace into which American life has been driven by its own heedless vitality . . . the writings of a culture that does not even know it is choking on exhaust fumes . . . a culture desperately clinging to the idea of value while vulgarizing almost every particular value . . . the American mobility culture, with its autos, obsolete and crunchable the day they're sold, its fast-food parlors, plastic motel rooms, take-out orders, transient sex and junk music."

It should not take a movie to convince a New Yorker that our national way of life is in disrepair. Only the cranky critics Rex Reed and Robert Mazzocco writing in the *New York Review of Books* suggested that it is not the people of *Nashville* that are shallow, but the movie itself. Mazzocco cautioned, *"Nashville,* I suspect, is an artificial high—a symptom of the disease and not a diagnosis of it." Both Bruce Cook in the *National Observer* and Nik Cohn in *New Times* developed this point, observing that the movie panders to the shared prejudices of movie reviewers and audiences. Cohn continued, "Now that blacks are sacrosanct, rednecks and hillbillies are the only real butts that hip Northerners

New York Times *Associate Editor Tom Wicker stated that* Nashville *depicts the "vulgarity, greed, deceit, cruelty, barely contained hysteria, and the frantic lack of root and grace into which American life has been driven by its own heedless vitality . . . ."*

have left. Niggers of the seventies, they can be parodied, mocked in absolute chic safety." Director Altman "cloaks his contempt in the trappings of sympathy, concern, understanding. Just like Hollywood coons in the thirties, his characters are permitted sorrows, a certain mute pathos. But that is their limit: he gives them no brain, and not the remotest talent."

This movie is neither America nor Nashville for two reasons. First, the film fails in its use of the *King Kong* strategy mentioned earlier. Showing a number of surfaces of a single subject might create a view of its deeper structure. To look—no matter how long or accurately—at one surface, however, cannot accomplish this end.

This problem is nicely illustrated in the role of the loose-jawed BBC reporter. With several other commentators, Vincent Canby of the *New York Times* believes that, unlike the other portrayals, the reporter is "idiotically gross" and "the film's single miscalculation." However, her part is no more gross than that of the other characters. Always asking, never listening, always recording (whether in bed with Don Juan or alone among mountains of junked cars), she mouths cosmopolitan preconceptions about the South as the last great frontier of a lost paradise. Always in quest of a story, she is the only one of the twenty-four principal characters who misses the assassination, the single news event of the movie. Geraldine Chaplin, who played the BBC reporter, wrote her own dialogue. It is certainly a parody of journalists; is it also a critique of the movie's creators, Altman and screenwriter Joan Tewkesbury? Overlooking the brutality in the film, only a performer's affectionate love for her two deaf children shakes and bewilders the reporter. Like the architects of the movie, and the "fear and loathing" crowd, she has not the slightest comprehension of what forces give meaning and dignity to the daily lives of most Americans and power country music.

Rather than revel in a romance of national self-hatred, Altman should have used his prodigious skills of filmcraft to ask how people seek and find meaning in their lives. Nashville and the country music dream factory are a perfect setting to place this quest, but the movie's single-dimension strategy has foredoomed the project to failure. It is not the single surface of pretense but the heartfelt struggles of temptation and guilt and good and evil, it is the struggle of old and new musical styles for market distance, it is the problem of sex, alcohol, employment, affluence, religion, and how to explain it all to the kids, that makes country music commercial and the flawed lives of its stars heroic in the eyes of millions.

Nashville is not America for a second reason: it is without some of the most important actors. The players engage in a pell-mell romp for five days, but who pulls the strings? Why do they run so hard? In a way this movie is like Altman's earlier success, *M.A.S.H.,* but there the context was well known. The actors were caught in a mindless bureaucratic war machine in which the U.S. Army pretended to be a United Nations policeman. The audience also viewed the movie at a time of growing doubts about U.S. involvement in the Vietnam conflict.

Nashville does not portray the institutional underpinnings of the music industry, and the audience cannot be presumed to know them. The music may be *displayed* at Opryland and the bars of lower Broadway, but is *made* on and around 16th Avenue South—music row, the province of RCA, MCA, CBS, WSM, BMI, CMA, MGM, ABC, Capitol, and the rest. This other American story of Nashville deals with how corporations, big and small, build people, use them, and then discard them. It deals with the ways in which corporate interests so often come before the interests even of the people making corporate decisions. One could hardly expect a thorough analysis since surprisingly little is understood about the role—both intended and unintended—of corporations in shaping the production of modern culture; but they *are* omnipresent. Not done in ignorance, the elimination of all corporate actors from the movie had to be deliberate obfuscation, unforgivable for a director who has spent his work life in movies and television.

In the way the movie was made, too, *Nashville* is a symptom rather than a diagnosis of the disease. Rather than use the wealth and diversity of songs and singers in Nashville who are affiliated with other record companies and publishers, every element of production was integrated so as to bring profit to ABC-Paramount, the firm releasing the film. Persons without recording contracts were employed to write and sing their own songs. These songs were assigned to a Paramount-owned publisher and the cast album released on ABC records. While there is a *sense* of widespread TV coverage in the film, all the TV equipment was from WNGE, the Nashville ABC affiliate. Johnny Carson, who routinely plugs RCA and NBC products, did nothing to promote this film when it was released.

In at least two senses, Loretta Lynn was right when she commented that Altman apparently "could not afford real stars." Using performers contracted to several corporations would have made for numerous inter-corporate difficulties and dissipated profits. Also, "real stars" would have written parts for themselves quite at variance with the unidimensional ethos of the movie. It could not then have been such a fine gloss of escapist entertainment, a pretended hard look at ourselves on the brink of the Bicentennial.

Chinatown

William Walling

Roman Polanski's *Chinatown* is such a clever pastiche of the best detective films of the 1940s, and it offers such thorough enjoyment in its own right through the departures it makes from those earlier films—most notably in the superb color photography by John Alonzo—that it is unlikely most viewers will bother to notice how much the film provides an implicit explanation for the devitalization of one of the more significant genres in our recent popular culture, not to speak of the way that genre was itself a kind of crude commentary on the vision we once had of ourselves as city dwellers.

The central plot in Robert Towne's highly competent screenplay is the scheme by which an already very wealthy man plans to realize an enormous profit in real estate through the manipulation of the Los Angeles water supply. It is a plot idea for which Towne seems to have found his inspiration in an actual episode from the mottled history of Los Angeles' growth: the Owens River Valley scandal of the earlier part of this century, a scandal whose complexities stretched themselves across more than two decades of city history.

In 1904, with Los Angeles parched to desperation by a severe and prolonged drought, William Mulholland, the superintendent of water, conceived the idea of a bold aqueduct system to carry the water of the Owens River from the eastern foothills of the Sierra Nevadas to the heart of the city. Supported by $25 million in bond issues, Mulholland was eventually to bring his dream to completion, presiding over the official opening of the aqueduct in 1913. Long before he did, however, the profiteering in San Fernando Valley land values by a syndicate that included Henry E. Huntington revealed the seamy underside of civic virtue. For the syndicate had learned of Mulholland's plan well before the public did (indeed, one member of the syndicate was on the Board of Water Commissioners), had recognized how the San Fernando Valley would be

Not only does Chinatown *cleverly imitate the central tensions of films like* The Maltese Falcon *and* The Big Sleep, *it also offers an implicit explanation for the decline of the genre itself—the continued reckless expansion of our cities through motives no more enlightened than the calculations of economic self-interest.*

transformed by the aqueduct into an almost incredibly fertile region, and had bought up more than 16,000 acres in the Valley—*at $30 an acre*—during the period that Mulholland's plan was still a virtual secret. It was, in short, a typical chapter of urban growth infiltrated by human greed; and if the details of this particular chapter are a little more highly colored than the usual accounts of insiders' manipulations in our cities' histories, one can probably explain the difference away by referring to the California locale, where events are always threatening to take on the slightly askew heightening of a technicolor fantasy.

Chinatown bears some interesting resemblances to this cause célèbre in Los Angeles history. For one, the city through which Jack Nicholson moves (as J. J. Gittes, private eye) is a landscape drying out under the ravages of a severe water shortage. For another, the scheme in *Chinatown* by which thousands of acres of farmland outside the city limits are being bought up at drought-stricken prices seems little more than a melodramatic updating of the plan that realized so great a profit in the San Fernando Valley at the turn of the century. Yet there are differences as well from this actual episode in Los Angeles history—not the least of which is Towne's (and Polanski's) decision to cast the action in the 1930s; a brief survey of the genre to which *Chinatown* belongs shows why the updating makes such good sense and at the same time indicates Towne's (and Polanski's) shrewdness in refusing to bring the action any closer to the present than the movie does, with its FDR posters and its four-door convertibles.

A recent remark of Ross Macdonald's helps to make this point clear. Commenting on his own views of the history of hardboiled fiction, Macdonald offered the suggestion that "much of the modern development of the detective story stems from Baudelaire . . . . [from] his vision of the city as inferno"—a remark that takes on a real suggestiveness if we consider the two writers Macdonald had most in mind in connection with his own work: Dashiell Hammett and Raymond Chandler. For in a crude sort of way, somewhere near the middle of the journey between art and schlock, the embattled private eye of classic hardboiled fiction really does become an emblem of psychic survival in the "inferno" of the modern city. In order to preserve himself intact (or so the code developed between Hammett's *Maltese Falcon* of 1930 and Raymond Chandler's *Long Goodbye* of 1953) the hardboiled detective had no choice but to remain a loner in the midst of people, relying on nothing so securely as his own wit and boldness, walking a personal tightrope between the powerful and the powerless, guarding himself incessantly against the sycophancies and delusions of the faceless crowd.

No doubt the most naked rendering of the code was in Hammett's depiction of Sam Spade in 1930—a depiction given enormously enlarged public exposure eleven years later through John Huston's choice of the then far-from-famous Humphrey Bogart for the leading role in the 1941 (and third) film version of *The Maltese Falcon.* For more than one generation of Americans, of course, it was the true beginning of a screen presence that was eventually to take on the dimensions of a myth—the craggy face, the grating voice, the cynicism that seemed to rest mysteriously on some kind of ideal (who knew what ideal?)—and I suspect most people forget too easily how little sentimentality there was in that earliest of Bogart's full-scale screen performances.

Yet it is hard to imagine a more entertaining deflation of sentimental expectations than the final episode of *The Maltese Falcon,* where Bogart-Spade tells the murderous Brigid O'Shaughnassy (Mary Astor) that he's going to turn her over to the police even though he loves her—for nobody, but *nobody,* played Sam Spade for a "sap." And in that climactic moment, as the camera centered on Spade's hard face, and then on Brigid's stunned one, it was as if the American film had finally been able to create an urban hero to rank with the legendary horsemen of the Hollywood West—the Tom Mixes and the William S. Harts, the William Boyds and the Gary Coopers.

Even more important, this new hero, unlike those earlier horsemen, was capable of dealing with at least something of the actual psychological tensions an urban audience knew. And of not merely dealing with them. For Bogart-Spade also suggested the possibility for a different, more humanely satisfying mode of behavior. It was, to be sure, a continued form of alienation that the image conveyed; but now it was an alienation raised to the level of a desperately logical kind of heroism: the isolated urban man with neither power nor money who still refuses to bend to the sentimentalities that the lack of power and money induces.

What seems most interesting about that image today, however, is the way in which history proceeded to undermine it almost as soon as it was formed. Nine weeks after *The Maltese Falcon* opened in New York, Pearl Harbor was bombed; and although it would be a patent absurdity to make too much of the image cast by only a single performer in our popular culture, the transformation within one year of the hardboiled loner of Huston's *Maltese Falcon* into the sentimental altruist of Curtiz's *Casablanca* of 1942 (with Bogart-Rick at the close of the later film bravely watching the climbing airplane as it carried Ingrid Bergman farther and farther from him, to the Free World) does provide a crudely obvious suggestion of the altered priorities of a nation at war. Indeed when John Huston did go on to make his first considerable film after the war had ended, *The Treasure of the Sierra Madre* (1948), the bravura performance at the center of it seemed like nothing so much as a palinode to the intense individualism that had animated *The Maltese Falcon*. For in place of the Bogart-Spade vitality of 1941 there was now the Bogart-Dobbs morbidity of 1948, a morbidity that revealed itself to be the madness and self-destructiveness inherent in the individualism of the prewar era.

Certainly the kind of unreflective individualism that lay at the heart of *The Maltese Falcon* could hardly remain unaffected by the transformations World War II brought about in our social landscape: not only the commonplace that the War "took us out of the Depression" but also the fact that the growth of the defense industries in many of our larger cities resulted in a significant alteration in racial balances and expectations. In Los Angeles for example—the setting both for *Chinatown* and for the Philip Marlowe novels of Raymond Chandler—the number of blacks more than doubled during the war years, from something like 70,000 in 1939 to approximately 150,000 by 1945, and many of these new arrivals came with the hope of getting some kind of defense work.

The decision to cast the action of Chinatown *in the 1930s makes far more esthetic sense than the usual flight into nostalgia that has characterized so many of our recent films. For the Los Angeles that Nicholson-Gittes travels across is really the unified city where hardboiled detective fiction has always been most at home.*

Such a large-scale phenomenon could not help but alter the psychological and moral terrain for anyone who already knew Los Angeles. And I suspect that it is this fact, more than any other, that helps to explain the curiously elegiac quality to the writing of Raymond Chandler. In Chandler's *The Little Sister* of 1949, he laments (sentimentally to be sure) the passing of the virtues of small-town America. But within the context of the genre in which it occurs, this lament also helps to illuminate the dilemma a writer like Chandler faced because of the social changes brought about by the Second War.

Aesthetically, the dilemma of the 1940s was that of the enormous difficulty of continuing to suggest, through the adventures of a single private eye, an actual urban landscape, since the kind of moral experience our urban landscapes were becoming could not longer easily be suggested by the traditional metaphor of the private eye's isolated vision. Many years later in 1966, after the convulsions of the Watts riots had made manifest the disastrous fragmentation of our urban life, Thomas Pynchon saw the racial sickness of Los Angeles as the coexistence of the two diverse cultures of black and white. He claimed that, "While the white culture is concerned with various forms of systematized folly . . . the black culture is stuck pretty much with basic realities like disease, like failure, violence and death, which the whites have mostly chosen—and can afford—to ignore."

This heightened awareness of racial separation that so characterized the 1960s was already accessible in the 1940s to a writer as intelligent as Chandler. The suggestion that arises is that the unified idea of the city that underlies a 1930 novel like *The Maltese Falcon* (and which Huston's film captured so well) was made possibly largely because of the narrow moral universe in which so much of hardboiled detective fiction happened to be written—a universe bounded by Prohibition on the one side and by a lingering Depression on the other. For Chandler, however, whose first novel did not appear until 1939 *(The Big Sleep),* the relative moral security of that universe had to absorb the shock of the tremendous social changes World War II brought about.

As a result we find that curious division of sensibility that is probably the most distinguishing feature of a Chandler novel. On the one hand there's the material drawn from the 1920s and 1930s, with its cheerfully uncomplicated emphasis on intrigues of simple-minded greed and adventure; on the other hand we can not help but notice how stoical and melancholy Marlowe really is, with his periodic retreats into the isolation of his lonely rooms, where he does nothing more than drink and play chess with himself.

By concentrating almost entirely on the qualities of Chandler's fiction that belonged most unambiguously to the 1930s, both Edward Dmytrk (with *Murder, My Sweet,* 1944) and Howard Hawks (with *The Big Sleep,* 1946) created films that rank with the best examples of the genre *Chinatown* imitates so cleverly. Nevertheless, there was something prophetic about the divided sensibility of Chandler's novels. And by the time the fourth film based on his fiction had been made—John Brahm's *Brasher Doubloon* of 1947—the loss of vitality was already evident across the entire genre.

Any number of films could be cited since that time to illustrate the genre's precipitous decline into pointless triviality or overt sensationalism. For the moral resonance that the idea of the private eye had once possessed—as an emblem for the isolated sensibility imposing some kind of humanly responsible order upon the apparent chaos of a credible urban landscape—that idea was overwhelmed by the moral complexities that an actual urban landscape increasingly suggested.

Gordon Parks's *Shaft* of 1971 and Robert Altman's *The Long Goodbye* of 1973 each recently attempted to update the genre in a strikingly different way. In the first, John Shaft (played by Richard Roundtree) is a tough, hip New York private eye who just happens to be black—in short, a spade Spade, as the script itself made clear. And the film takes off from that premise: that here and now, in the eighth decade of the twentieth century, the corruption and danger of urban America can only be confronted in all its diversity by a black updating of Hammett's Spade. Yet the concept of John Shaft really had no more relationship to the actual moral complexities of our time than the impotent projections of an adolescent fantasy.

As for *The Long Goodbye,* Altman's approach was to give the hedonistic side of Los Angeles, with Elliot Gould cast as a Philip Marlowe appropriate for the 1970s—that is, as a Philip Marlowe who behaved as if he had been popping amphetamines since the opening of *The Brasher Doubloon* in 1947. It was, to be sure, an up-to-the-moment Los Angeles that Altman showed us—or at least what we were allowed to see of the city seemed up to the moment. But *The Long Goodbye* was so clearly a film that dealt only with the white, affluent—and dizzily empty—side of Los Angeles that the final effect was of camp rather than drama. Both *Shaft* and *The Long Goodbye,* in their divergent attempts to put a private eye into the inferno of a contemporary urban landscape, could do no better than reflect the distortions at either end of a profound cultural separation. And the result in both cases was essentially the same: the aesthetic feebleness of an incompletely grasped subject, so that *Shaft* dissolved into the silliness of weak fantasy, *The Long Goodbye* into the flaccid amorality of camp.

The decision to cast the action of *Chinatown* in the 1930s, then, makes far more aesthetic sense than the usual flight into nostalgia that has characterized so many of our recent films. For the Los Angeles that Nicholson-Gittes travels across is really the unified city where hardboiled detective fiction has always been most at home. Thus a polite Chicano boy on a burro helpfully answers Gittes's questions, providing him with the necessary information for reconstructing the scheme by which the city's water supply is being diverted. (By way of historic contrast, white Los Angeles' treatment of its Mexican-American community in the early 1940s surely ranks among the shabbiest chapters in the city's history, culminating as it did in the so-called Zoot-Suit Riots of June 1943, when white police and servicemen conspired to brutalize just about every Chicano male they could get their hands on.) A deferential Japanese gardener keeps saying "glass" for "grass" to the inquisitive Gittes, and thus supplies him with a kind of zany subliminal clue for the eventual discovery of a pair of bifocals in a garden pool. (I don't think I have to specify how Los Angeles treated its Japanese residents during the early 1940s.)

Indeed, even the title *Chinatown*—as the place, we learn in the film, "where anything can happen"—is meant to suggest an implicit community of shared experience. For in the film's final episode all of the major characters (almost all of them white) encounter each other on Chinatown's main avenue, where the unexpectedly violent "anything" of a supposedly alien culture is exactly what happens to the major characters. And as the film trails off to its ending after this burst of violence, our eyes are unavoidably directed to J. J. Gittes walking slowly away from us in the distance, headed now even more deeply into the heart of Chinatown, the classic private eye of the thirties and forties divorced once more from the hope of love.

It is the kind of close that makes it easy enough to guess what general effect Polanski is aiming for: the evocation of a sense of loss for our having traveled so far with the fundamental decency of J. J. Gittes's private vision—only to see that private vision overwhelmed (as it never was overwhelmed in the films of the forties) by a triumphantly funky evil, personified by John Huston's Noah Cross. Moreover, as previously suggested, the scheme of land-profiteering at the center of *Chinatown* foreshadows nothing so clearly as the continued expansion of Los Angeles. And it is this continued expansion of Los Angeles that will eventually undermine the hypothetical one-city atmosphere that *Chinatown* constructs so carefully. (Nowhere in the film, for example, do we encounter the presence of a black population; and there is even a moment, near the start of Gittes's investigation, where we seem to be back in nineteenth-century America, at a townhall meeting, as irate farmers drive a flock of sheep up the center aisle during a public hearing of the Los Angeles Water Commission.)

For that reason, Polanski deserves credit for having given us something a good deal more interesting than the merely affectionate re-creation of an earlier generation's successes in the hardboiled detective genre. For not only does *Chinatown* cleverly imitate the central tensions of films like *The Maltese Falcon* and *The Big Sleep,* it also offers an implicit explanation for the decline of the genre itself—the continued reckless expansion of our cities through motives no more enlightened than the calculations of economic self-interest.

That such an explanation is hardly adequate for the decline either of our cities or of hardboiled detective fiction really does not matter. Nor does it seem especially important that for a vision of apocalyptic evil Polanski can do no better than present John Huston in a very broad performance as a patriarchal robber baron who believes that sex is best if it stays in the family. What is of interest is the way Polanski makes use of a scheme for urban expansion to suggest a distinctive aesthetic effect: the simultaneous celebration—and symbolic interment—of the genre that is his subject. Hence, at the close of *Chinatown* I suspect we are intended to experience something more than merely a sense of J. J. Gittes's personal defeat. Rather, as Nicholson-Gittes walks away from us, into the gathering night, it is as if we are watching the forward movement of the archetypal private eye into the darkness of oblivion, overwhelmed by history and by the oncoming moral chaos of our postwar cities.

Yet even if we do grant all of this to Polanski, the sad fact remains that *Chinatown* is not more than a distinctly minor work. For although it is the movie of 1974 that I would recommend to just about everyone for a pleasantly exciting two hours, *Chinatown* finally can not escape the weight of the history it seems so cleverly to evade. We know too sharply that a bit of moral legerdemain is going on; we can not help but sense how much the film is constantly being diminished by the absence of risk its 1930s setting implies. And it is this, ultimately, that demonstrates the interment of the genre in a much cruder fashion than any of the subtle requiem services Polanski may have wanted to suggest. The eye, in short, for all the brilliance of Jack Nicholson's performance as J. J. Gittes, looks out upon the desert landscape of a dishonestly contrived past.

All in the Mafia Family: *The Godfather*

Isidore Silver

Eric Hobsbawm, in his classic *Primitive Rebels,* says of the Sicilian Mafia, "In lawless communities power is rarely scattered among an anarchy of competing units, but clusters around local strong-points" and "Its typical form is patronage." The myth-opera-fable of the movie *The Godfather* (an infinitely superior pop art version of its clumsy novelistic predecessor) is little more than a gloss upon Hobsbawn's thesis. What makes *The Godfather* of special interest however is neither the relevance of that thesis to America nor the esthetic quality of the movie, but rather the virtually unanimous, almost mindless acclaim it has received from both credulous audiences and flaccid critics. As with *Patton* two years ago, the picture seems to appeal to almost every segment of our fractured society. Why such accolades for what is only after all another (though well done) American gangster movie? Do we feel ourselves to be members of a lawless community, a pre-modern or a pre-industrial primitive Ardrey-like society? To fend off the anarchy of competing units, do we seek local strong-points? An analysis of both the picture and the book (which differ in several crucial respects) may provide some of the answers to these intriguing questions.

The Godfather is an epic novel recited in flat, narrative prose and is given a "classical"—spare, stately and traditional—screen treatment. The heroes (and whatever the reservations of Puzo and Coppola, heroes they are) are not merely men who scheme, connive, and double-cross; they are larger than life, their emotions purer and more volatile than those experienced by the rest of us. Like classical gods, they are in the world but not of it. The titanic emotions of the novel (as befitting an epic, they are stated, not described) are perfectly captured by Puzo's declamatory description of Sonny Corleone's (son and heir apparent to Don Vito) decision to wipe out his enemies: "Perhaps it was the

The Corleone family is understood by no one and it has no wish to participate in the public affairs of men. All other species of human beings are either abstract (that vaguely described Jewish judge, that unknown kept congressman) or subhuman (those "nigger animals" for whom drugs are too benign a fate).

stalemate that made Sonny . . . embark on the bloody course of attrition that ended in his own death. Perhaps it was his dark violent nature given full reign.''

The Corleone family is understood by no one and it has no wish to participate in the public affairs of men. All other species of human being are either abstract (that vaguely described Jewish judge, that unknown kept congressman) or subhuman (those "nigger animals" for whom drugs are too benign a fate). Occasionally, a WASP such as Kay Adams (who becomes Michael Corleone's wife and—in the novel though not the movie—a good Catholic to boot) or Tom Hagan, the Godfather's *consigliere* (a quasi-Sicilian by informal adoption) slips into the mosaic, but the general atmosphere is that of a stiflingly closed society characterized by eternal interfamilial warfare. Apart from titanic wars and unending displays of patronage, the Mafia seems to do very little. Because they work so hard, the gods must often rest.

The irrelevance of society in general is best demonstrated by the fact that all of the killings save two are of Sicilians. A famous Mafia biography was entitled *We Only Kill Each Other,* and the movie reassures us that these gods, though indeed warlike, are not very dangerous to us. The movie eliminates all of the book's references to outsiders such as the Jewish doctor who marries the ex-mistress of the heroic, foolish, and ultimately martyred Sonny; the only two Jews of any prominence, Moe Bloom (an apparent combination of the real life Bugsy Siegel and Moe Dalitz) and Jack Woltz (a *ganef* movie producer) are disposed of— Bloom is killed—with dispatch and only because they presented minor impediments to the Family.

The Godfather also has more mundane progenitors, namely the traditional gangster and Western genres. Both traditions, whatever their differences, exemplify the same myth—the myth of the non-existence of civilized society. As Hobsbawn says, when "the official government could not or would not exercise effective sway, the appearance of [lawless local groups] was as inevitable as the appearance of gang-rule, or its alternative, private posses and vigilantes in certain parts of *laissez-faire* America.'' The movie makes clear that the official government cannot govern—in the first scene, Angelo Bonasera has placed his trust in the courts and has not found justice for his daughter (assaulted by two boys) and so begs Don Vito to exact private vengeance. After castigating Bonasera for deigning to trust civil authorities, the Don grants the wish. Michael Corleone, Don Vito's second son and successor Don (after he has proved his worth by annihilating the Family's current enemies), at one point in the novel sums up the nature of Hobbesian Society (the war of all against all) by saying, "Society doesn't really protect its members who do not have their own individual power."

The moral ambiguity of the hero in all of those James Cagney and Edward G. Robinson gangster movies (In *Little Caesar,* Robinson, dying, incredulously and heartrendingly gasps, "Is this the end of Rico?") is amply reflected in *The Godfather.* There are, after all, good and bad Godfathers—the good one (Brando as Vito Corleone) doesn't want to go into drugs (though he disclaims any moral motives) while the evil one (Richard Conte as Barzini) does. Although all moral problems in the movie are treated as business, the audience is encouraged to identify with Brando and to sanction the assassination of Conte (who not only deals in drugs, but smiles and ridicules the solemnity of Brando's funeral—an incident not found in the book).

Other traditions feed in to *The Godfather.* The sets, the lighting, and the hyper-intense conversations all suggest opera. Indeed, one has the impression that the move is a dress rehearsal for an opera without music. At times the similarity becomes almost ludicrous. In one climactic scene, Michael is in church blessing his sister's baby as a godfather while his henchmen are settling scores with the Barzini gang; the pounding organ on the soundtrack and the crosscutting on screen heighten the tension between Michael's confession and absolution on the one hand and the slaughter on the other until the grandiosity threatens to drown itself in *opéra bouffe.* The picture's operatic quality is enhanced by its uncanny resemblance to Luchino Visconti's memorable saga of another pre-industrial family trying to adjust to modern life, *Rocco and His Brothers.* Indeed, much of *The Godfather* looks like Visconti's *Damned* while the dialogue sounds like *Rocco.*

Although the mixture of epic, tale, and opera is esthetically pleasing, the question of the intellectual and psychological appeal of *The Godfather* remains. Of course, it perpetuates the myth that the Mafia is a pervasive social and political presence in American life (only a few Treasury agents and FBI men seem immune to its influence). The movie takes the myth for granted—presumably so does the audience—and omits the furtive meetings, smashing exposes and appropriate comeuppances so characteristic of the Mafia subclass of the Hollywood gangster genre. Of course, that myth has been the essence of popular conceptions of the Mafia for at least a decade (or two, depending upon whether one's political virginity was terminated by Joseph Valachi or by Estes Kefauver) and has furnished numerous political rationales for a panoply of repressive legislation (such as "liberal" wiretap laws) which never seem to be sufficient to solve the problem of "organized crime."

The myth is of course questionable and the movie raises—but does not resolve—one particular contradiction. We learn that the Corleone family is the only one (at least in the New York area) that seems to enjoy high political influence; the major conflict starts when other families want to appropriate such influence to facilitate the buildup of the drug trade. If money is the great equalizer, at least to non-Sicilian society as the movie generally argues, then why can't it be utilized by the Barzini family? The differences between the Good Don and the Bad Don (see myth number two above) obviously account for the differences in political clout. But the combination of the myths, while making each more palatable to the audience, unfortunately runs counter to Lord Acton's dictum that power corrupts and absolute power corrupts absolutely. That estimable assessment was, of course, shared by Machiavelli, the Godfather's Godfather —but the movie, in its desire to make the Mafia look bad but not too bad, equivocates at this vital point.

Since Americans believe in Reason and Progress, the myth of the mysterious Mafia exercising virtually plenary power of society is particularly appropriate. Governmental ineptitude becomes explainable as a species of corruption and corruption is understandable as a different form of rationality. The myth reinforces the cynical side of our supposedly ruggedly individualistic natures and demonstrates that the public interest is nothing more than political rhetoric. If such an interest cannot, in the nature of things, exist, then why not admit it and let politically rational man amass as much power as he (or his family) can. To liberals, the Mafia can replace the "malefactors of great wealth" as the villains while conservatives can now rail at something besides welfare "handouts." For the powerless, in the words of the novel, "there comes a time when the most humble of men, if he keeps his eyes open, can take his revenge on the most powerful." Something for everyone, except for the occasional believer in the possibilities of collective social action.

The movie explains the anarchy of modern life. If, in Hobsbawm's words, "the Mafia maintained public order by private means," then, to an extent, the movie Mafia is doing the same thing. Discipline among the troops, cooperation with others (where necessary) are the watchwords of the Family. Peacefulness and social cooperation, two major avowed ends of organized society, are reflected in the incessant attempts by the Corleone family to negotiate new truces, to make generous offers to those enterprises they wish to acquire, and to insure a minimum of governmental interference in their form of free enterprise. In contrast to the private banditti roaming the American city-scape, murder is only "business" to the Mafia (and only Sicilian business at that).

The complexities and uncertainties of modern life are reduced by the Mafia. Problems are readily solved—kill the head man. Institutions have

The Godfather *appeals to certain middle-American (and not only middle-American) fantasies. The family is still the integral unit of society; people must marshall their own power and cannot cooperate with outsiders; each man has a mystical destiny and everyone else—including social institutions—had better get out of the way of the fulfillment of that destiny.*

no meaning, only people do—that is the great wisdom which facilitated the rise of Don Vito (a critical part of the novel details that rise, but in the movie the mythic Brando exists with no background, in no temporal dimension). Of course long range planning, if properly applied, can reduce the instability and unforeseeability of life. Tom Hagan forecasts the plans of rival families for a full ten years with an accuracy that would warm the heart of Jay Forrester and his MIT computers. Michael, when he becomes head of the family, tells his wife that they will become wholly legitimate in three to five years.

The foregoing, then, means that men can affect events. Powerful institutions can be controlled and, in place of faceless bureaucrats, we can have an eminently approachable leader—the Don—who will listen to supplicants and make proper decisions (at some cost, but what doesn't involve some cost?). Thus, the *volk,* swearing allegiance to the person of a leader, will be served by an instinctive communion which needs no (and even transcends) legal forms (and if Hannah Arendt's characterization of the Nazi oath to Hitler in *Origins of Totalitarianism* seems strangely relevant, then so be it). The Family becomes the organ through which community participation in relevant decisions occurs and only the recalcitrant will ask whether the Don may not always be wise, especially when the exercise of his wisdom cannot be subjected to questioning or appeal.

While the romanticism which attaches to the Mafia will doubtlessly proceed apace, it overlooks the fundamental relationship between that group and the Establishment we all (for varying reasons, to be sure) despise. As Richard Nixon's freeing of Jimmy Hoffa demonstrates in another context, the Establishment and the deviant (if the latter is part of a powerful organization) find areas of mutual accommodation. Michael, during his exile in Sicily, ironically observes that the Sicilian Mafia "had become a degenerate capitalist structure" and "cancerous to the society it inhabited." Presumably Puzo was aware, in some way, of Hobsbawn's assertion that "gangsters have a vested interest in private property" and that "the chief tendency of Mafia's development is away from a social movement and towards at best a political pressure group and at worst a complex of extortion rackets." By the end of both novel and movie, it is evident that Don Michael hopes to accomplish the former but the direction of his leadership will insure the latter. He will not be legitimate in three to five years—or indeed ever.

It becomes apparent (though the movie would never dare suggest it) that while the Corleones may have gained strength from a credulous peasantry (or neo-peasantry), their identification will inevitably be with conservative propertied classes. As Hobsbawm says of the Neapolitan *Camorra,* the organization will become the "secret police of the State against Liberals" and "like all professional criminals, it has a bias towards private property as a system." The Neo-Populist bias of the movie is egregiously misplaced.

/Finally, *The Godfather* appeals to certain middle-American (and not only middle-American) fantasies. The family is still the integral unit of society; people must marshal their own power and cannot cooperate with outsiders; each man has a mystical destiny and everyone else—including social institutions—had better get out of the way of fulfillment of that destiny. If Ayn Rand's Howard Ruark was justified in blowing up a building to fulfill his destiny only a niggler would complain about *The*

Godfather's sanction of slightly more extreme violence. The critical line in the novel about the difference between the Family and society is a mocking reference to the judge who suspends the sentence upon the two men who attacked Angelo Bonasera's daughter: "The law in its majesty does not seek vengeance." Perhaps many of us believe that the law should, with or without majesty, seek exactly that and that no quibbling about individual rights should stand in its way. But what if opposing concepts of justice are present, what if each side has a claim to justice (and indeed each defines the term differently)? No such thing exists in the moral universe of *The Godfather*.

Both the movie and the novel are successful in part because the Mafia is perceived as offering no real threat to middle America. Michael, after all, wants his kids "to grow up to be all-American kids, real all-American, the whole works." The ethic of Family, Honor, Loyalty and Hard Work is strictly from Consciousness I. *The Godfather* is not important for the validity of its views about the Mafia; much contradictory evidence abounds to support any of three beliefs—that the Cosa Nostra a) still exists in much the same form as it did in the forties, b) is dying as an illegal institution and its energies are being diverted into legal channels and c) is not, and never was, an important constituent of either organized crime or American life. *The Godfather* institution (for that is what it has become) is significant because of its appeal to an aspect—one aspect—of the American character at this point in history. That appeal raises the question of whether large segments of the society have withdrawn from any belief in the possibilities of public action, have rescinded the moral authority underlying the welfare state and have sanctioned a regression to pre-industrial modes of social relationships—what might be called the "Sicilianization" of American life. Perhaps we will comprehend more about this when the musical version of *The Godfather* opens on Broadway.

The Overdeveloped Society: *THX1138*

Bernard Beck

Science fiction cannot be taken seriously without accepting it on its own terms—as entertainment. Some serious thinkers have used it as a way of making serious points (George Orwell, H. G. Wells, Aldous Huxley), but the corpus of works in the genre is more significant than the individual attempts to exploit it for a political or philosophical message. It obviously lends itself especially well to utopian thinking, to emphasizing long-term consequences of current trends and to commenting on the relation of technology to human life. But when the message precedes the expression in science fiction terms, the result rarely swings as well as when involvement in the world of "sci-fi" generates a message.

The genre, as opposed to any particular creator within it, has an implicit logic and set of themes and issues which are interesting in themselves. The ingenuity and insight which may impress the casual audience with a serious lesson will strike the aficionado as quite conventional, familar from many previous examples of simple escapism. This is the "error" of crediting to a particular specimen the excellence of the type. Thus, there can be no discussion of a heavy specimen which is not based on a knowledge of the context.

Familiarity begins with an appreciation of the special appeal of science fiction, which is an experience not completely reducible to analysis. Anyone who doesn't have the taste for it will find it hard to like *THX 1138*. I have the taste, and I liked the movie; that is the premise of this discussion. It was a pleasure to sit and watch the movie. Not everyone will feel that way, and anyone who doesn't is unlikely to find any other kind of significance it may have redeeming.

As in the classic detective story, the most important feature of science fiction is neither narrative nor character. The literary surface is imposed on what is basically a mental exercise. The starting point, of course, is an interest in science (usually but not always in the sense of technological innovation) and its unforeseen consequences. The fun part, though, is the process of generating the innovation and consistently following out the logic implied by it. The creator invites his audience to join him in a hypothetical game of "What if . . . ?" What matters most is starting with a provocative and novel hypothesis and milking it for all the surprising and ingenious things that would then probably be true. As in other such ventures (locked-room murder stories, code and cipher stories, crossword puzzles), the worth of the achievement is judged by the difficulty of the problem undertaken. Impressive science fiction therefore has to wrestle with mind-benders like time travel, parapsychology, cosmic history, new forms of energy or the mysteries of hyperspace. Finding a different kind of animal life on Mars is not the kind of thing that gets the science fiction fan very excited anymore, unless it includes some very novel twist of biology or social psychology.

Such mental games should be based on science. This proceeds from the desacralization and objectivization of nature and feels no compunction about rearranging things and imagining alternatives. People who enjoy the hypothetical activity of science fiction are close to understanding the character of scientific detachment, more a matter of temperament than philosophy. Thus, among the newer applications of science fiction are school exercises in functionalist sociology, architecture and city planning. This playful quality of science fiction is transformed by the addition of one element, a stake in the premise, which produces "message" science fiction. "What if . . . ?" becomes "Wouldn't it be wonderful if . . . ?" (utopianism like *Looking Backward)* or "Wouldn't it be terrible if . . . ?" (jeremiads like *1984).* The imposition of messages is similar to the contemporary concern with making technology more responsive to humane values and social control. We have yet to suggest a way of reconciling the moral constraints on technical development with the self-fulfillment of the unfettered scientist. Both science and science fiction are aristocratic pursuits, and we can understand why mathematicians are such whimsical people.

As science fiction matured, it became somewhat surfeited with the possibilities of material technology and more curious about social organizational consequences. The rise of this "social science fiction" has also accompanied the growth of social science in this century. Increasingly, science fiction has explored institutional arrangements and personality structures in its hypothetical futures. This has made it more interesting literarily *(Slaughterhouse Five),* more relevant politically *(Stranger in a Strange Land)* and more easily confused with ordinary fiction. It has also made it more difficult, in the same ways that social science is more difficult than the "hard" sciences. But since degree of difficulty is a positive value in science fiction, it has also gotten better.

If science fiction is an exploratory game, then there are good reasons why it is better when the morals emerge at the end than when they are imposed in front. If it has a value beyond itself, it is in the possibility that it will make clear the results we should have a moral opinion about. The values we insist on before we begin cannot, unfortunately, be discovered at the end. Just as in sociological theory, our value-premises may shape the possibilities we allow ourselves to see. An unexamined assumption about the future will confirm itself in the science fiction written on that assumption. So if we have such predispositions, we are always well advised to announce them, in science fiction as well as in science.

Science fiction is first of all a written form. Its most pleasing accomplishment is often nothing more than a language structure for describing events which are concretely unimaginable or meaningless in ordinary terms. First-rate science fiction often includes lengthy passages with no referential content, describing nonexistent theories or deriving logical conclusions from absurd axioms by preposterous rules. Paradoxically, the less content such an account has, the more impressive it is to the science fiction reader. Nothing pleases him more than the elaboration of a hypothetical reality based on a (for the time being) scientific absurdity.

Film science fiction presents substantively different problems from the written form, but it is comparable in the way it appeals to its audience. It is at once easier and more difficult. Science fiction movies are also based on the joy of working out "What if . . . ?", but in cinematic rather than wordy ways. It is easier because the eye is more easily pleased than the imagination. The visual realization of, say, the docking of the shuttle at the space station in the second segment of *2001* was satisfying in a way the verbal telling could not be. On the other hand the production of that image is a prodigious feat for the film-maker, while it is a small problem for the writer to indicate in a few sentences. Thus the shattering experience of the final segment of *2001* remains visually anticlimactic, in spite of Kubrick's best technical gimcrackery. So when the science fiction fan sees a movie, he looks for the same kind of excellence, but in a different form. It is the production, the creation of a concrete image of the impossible out of available techniques, that is the crucial factor. Film critics make the same error with such movies that literary critics make with science fiction novels. They dismiss too easily the mechanical problem-solving aspects and make demands of camera artistry, character, plot and theme. So *2001* has been the most underrated and most overrated of recent films because both critics and cultists believed that it was really about all those wordy apologies.

THX 1138 is set in a future (not very distant, it warns us) when technology allows a society of highly organized technical workers controlled by electronics and sedatives. This is one of the basic science-fiction premises as well as being a commonplace of mass society theorists.

In a way, the science fiction movie is one of the most purely cinematic of genres, depending for its life on the creation of a concrete reality in sight and sound. Whether this is done in a philosophical void, like a George Pal production, or in service to a humane theme, as in Fritz Lang's *Metropolis,* the final judgment rests on the emergence of meaning from the constructed reality of concrete images. For most of film history, success or failure has been the responsibility of set designers, special effects men, sound engineers and animationists. It is possible for a good movie to lack these contributions, just as a good novel about the future could be uninteresting to the science fiction reader. But it would then have to be considered as not belonging to the genre in any important sense. And a book or movie could be good both in science fiction and in literary terms, but there is no particular connection between the two achievements. In fact, a work that tries to do both is less likely to be wholly satisfying as either.

THX 1138 is very satisfying as science fiction and as a film, without being particularly innovative as either. Its literary character is more problematic, though still quite good enough for a movie; it is also highly derivative. So without being real news, the movie is a happy synthesis of high quality elements. For many people in the audience it will provide both a moving and original experience. The movie may show that the science fiction film has come of age, like the western. It has developed from juvenile space opera and pretentious allegory into a form whose basic conventions are understood by a sizable audience. So, like the western, we expect it not to be new but the same familiar thing well done. *THX 1138* is very well done.

It is set in a future (not very distant, it warns us) when technology allows a society of highly organized technical workers controlled by electronics and sedatives. This is one of the basic science fiction premises as well as being a commonplace of mass society theorists. Sophisticated technology produces totalitarian control, while the complexity and top-heaviness of the mass system requires high output from people in high-level alienated labor. Life is barren and cheerless in a synthetic environment, and personal space is virtually non-existent. THX 1138, the title character, is a machine doctor, working with high energy to repair robots. He is troubled because his computer-selected roommate, a woman, is substituting dummy capsules for his libido-suppressing sedative. She wants him, and he responds. Their love-making is a criminal antisocial act. The intrusion of a high-ranking fellow worker, a man, who wants THX for his own roommate, and THX's non-sedated shakiness at work get all three busted. He is "reconditioned" and held in detention, where he makes his escape with the other man. They join up with a black runaway (blacks are all used as performers on the hologram, 3-D television) and start running. From here on, the movie is a Great Escape. THX first looks for LUH, his lost love, but finds she has been "consumed." All the escapees fail, except THX, who finally climbs to the "superstructure" (surface of the Earth) because the organized pursuit has exceeded its budget and is called off as robot cops are closing in on him. In the closing shot, THX stands erect, silhouetted against a huge orange sun ball as a wild goose flies over.

The movie takes an appraoch to the visual production problem of science fiction which has been used to good effect in recent adult films in the genre. It is the exact opposite of the costly special effects and animation approach of *Destination Moon* and *2001*. It consists of constructing a future world completely out of contemporary elements in our world. The total absence of artifacts and images that are not contemporaneous produces a convincing futurism. We have seen this approach used in Godard's *Alphaville,* Truffaut's *Fahrenheit 451* and *The Tenth Victim.* The original discovery probably comes from Antonioni's *L'Avventura,* which was not about the future at all.

But is *THX 1138* about the future? A doctored trailer for an old Buck Rogers serial serves as preamble to the movie. The voice-over has Buck in the twentieth century, rather than the twenty-fifth. And we are informed that the important thing about Buck is that he is just an ordinary fellow like you and me, even though he lives in the marvelous "future." THX's world is extrapolated from current social trends and available technical possibilities. The movie is successful in creating a visual technological reality, but its point is political and cultural.

A special circumstance throws the sociological element into great prominence. This film is directly based on a celebrated student film done several years ago by its makers. That film presented only the escape and the chase, without any development of characters or plot. The action was seen through the eyes of the TV monitoring devices used to control the system. The film was more abstract, more intense and in many ways more effective. The device of showing a man's successful run for freedom through the perspective of his jailers produced a powerful thematic statement in cinematic terms so apt as to become a pun on the medium. It was a distillation of the basic form of the escape movie.

Escape movies are all alike, and we never tire of the similarity. They may vary a bit in establishing the nature of the confinement (prisons, POW camps, kidnappers, the Iron Curtain), the escapers and their motivations (love, sport, sublime love of freedom, fear of death), but we are in the theater to see Dick run. We may all be suckers to a nostalgic yearning to be free of our routine social bonds. Whatever our inner vulnerabilities are, our delight in seeing a man cheat the organized system of the compliance it has so carefully engineered is a fundamental form of political radicalism. By comparison with this political stance of escape movies in general, the specific political inventions of *THX 1138* are mere window dressing.

By a basic convention of science fiction, future technology produces totalitarianism by creating irresistible social control. A corollary shows that the outcome is the same for all forms of social organization, in particular for both capitalism and socialism. It is a kind of extrapolation from the conventional wisdom of sociology about the structural uniformities of all industrial societies. *THX 1138* shows a world where organizational scale and the drive for material productivity have achieved the consequences predicted by Paul Goodman and Herbert Marcuse for capitalist society. Yet, the film-makers give symbolic indications that it is born of left-wing collectivism (a pseudoreligious, Cuban-bearded icon called Om; loudspeaker exhortations to serve the masses). A minor irony in the movie is the realization in its future world of many current movement goals, displayed in demonic form: the replacement of the nuclear family by the larger community as the effective unit of socialization, the open classroom, the material and symbolic equality of the sexes, planned fertility, the elimination of the private automobile, the institutionalization of altruism and equal opportunity. But because human scale has been exceeded, these victories become further forms of oppression.

The movie presents all the common forms of social control: the rationalization of physical space (in the superstate of the future, it has been agreed, we will live completely indoors), programmed learning of common ideologies (school subjects will be absorbed intravenously), monitoring of all human activity (TV, data banks, surveillance of brain functions), manipulation of human biochemistry (drug abuse means not taking your assigned doses), suppression of libido, ventilation of frustrations in the confessional, mass media propaganda and repressive desublimation, centralized control of the distribution of the means of survival and, for comic relief, robot cops in crash helmets and motorcycle jackets. There is some ingenuity in the social-science-fiction devices; the solutions are cute, like the role of black people or how a prison is run.

There is one major feature which is arbitrarily chosen, the management of sexuality. Creators of totalitarian futures in science fiction have been of two minds about the connection of sexuality to social control. One school, represented by *1984*, holds that sexuality will be suppressed as a threat to good order. The other, as in *Brave New World*, sees sexuality as the new opium of the people, diverting their attention from thoughts of liberation. *THX 1138* opts for the first hypothesis and, in keeping with that choice, gives the outbreak of sexual love as the seed of rebellion and finally escape. It may occur to other viewers that by using sexuality, rather than suppressing it, the engineers of this future world could have saved themselves some trouble. There would remain the problem of the productivity of labor, but in science fiction a little chemistry may properly be invoked to handle such difficulties.

THX 1138 has been less than imaginative in devising ways for this new society to seduce its members with mass-produced diversions. They are especially remiss because our contemporary society has already shown great ingenuity in that area. These future engineers seem to know less about gulling the masses than Madison Avenue does in the present. In particular, that strikingly collective society seems very short on collective institutions. There are no mass meetings, no rituals, no rallies. Perhaps American movie-makers, like other Americans, are still operating with an individualistic world view. Even in this beehive, they don't produce much that is convincingly social.

This point leads us to the real problem with the escape. Although we are ready to accept escape as its own good reason, escape movies seem always to construct a rationale for us. In this asocial movie, as in those social theories which overemphasize the state and thus neglect society, the only source of change is the mysterious hunger of the inaccessible body. In particular, the voracious womb of the natural female, as in mythology, subverts the social order. The girls have done it again! But this crude plot device is needed only when there is not recognition of a social dialectic.

Although four people are involved in the escape, THX, his girl friend LUH, his would-be roommate and the black performer, they remain strangers and their relationships are superficial. As each of the other three fail, in isolation and beyond mutual aid, THX directs himself to escape on his own, having transcended sex, friendship and brotherhood. But, in spite of the pessimism of this entire genre, it is time for greater sociological sophistication in social science fiction. It is time to develop the holes and anomalies which must characterize such a large social machine. We can be sure there will be wholesale evasions, criminal conspiracies, corruption in high places, waste and inefficiency, deviance, perversion, rebellion and every other variety of collective resistance to a collectivist organization. Escapes will come from social contact, not from isolation. There will be undergrounds, illicit parties, dirty songs and illegal purveyors. The one aspect which is promising in the movie, the illegitimate ability of a government official to rig the random housing assignments of the computer, is left unexamined. The only real evidence of the continued permeability of social structure is the abandonment of the chase because of a cost overrun.

Thus, THX does escape to the surface through a fluke in the system. The movie ends mercifully with his victorious moment of emergence. Yet, although he is free, he is alone and without consciousness. He really has nowhere to go.

Total Institutions on Celluloid: Wiseman Films

Chandra Hecht

Frederick Wiseman is a master filmmaker who chooses as subject matter those parts of organized social life which sociologists have called "total institutions." In *Titticut Follies, Law and Order, High School, Hospital* and *Basic Training,* he attempts to expand and explain his personal understanding of this aspect of society through the use of organized visual data.

Wiseman enters institutions such as hospitals and high schools with a medium that can convey ideas difficult to explain in words. He is forced to present visual relationships between situations and nonverbal communication in social interaction. And since the medium has the peculiar capacity to reveal day-to-day routines of institutions, Wiseman's films depict the charade-like qualities of life in institutions.

Wiseman's *Basic Training* is a trip into the esthetics of socialization. It is a study of that part of the army that recruits and trains its novices, but more than that it is about a dance (or more superficially a game) that the army has developed to teach and ready their future participants for a position within that institution's structure.

Like most institutions the army begins socializing recruits with status degradation ceremonies—Wiseman shows them getting uniforms, being fingerprinted and losing their hair. They become nobodies. The institution then provides them with an education that can give them a new identity. They learn 1) etiquette: how to address an officer, 2) a definition of their position within the institution: that they have the ability to fit in, 3) a description of their feelings: that they want to leave but it is too late, and 4) a new reality: that they are in an institution that claims to need them and defines itself as good. They are now inside novices.

The next film day is a full introduction to living in the institution. The novices get up, learn to brush their teeth, see how to clean the latrine and learn the basic exercises that will characterize the rest of their life in basic training—physical exercise, learning about weapons, hearing the ideology of the institution (that they will need to be able to kill because they are going to war), learning discipline and marching. And with the marching they learn a basic source of ideological training—the marching song, "Ain't no use in marching back."

The exercises that are intended to teach military skills actually foster the idea that masculine virility will result from the mastery of these techniques. The trainees learn to shoot rifles by watching a man shooting one from his thigh, his groin, his chin and finally from his chest on full automatic. All this is greeted with chuckles and gasps of awe. At the end the guns are checked for shells. One soldier, responding to his training, says "push it down there," as the rod goes into the gun.

These are the first two sequences of Wiseman's editing. He simultaneously shows the processing of the recruit through the institution, the dance of army socialization and the symbolic rewards that the recruit learns to want and that supposedly come with fitting into the institution. The medium, and the way Wiseman uses it, depicts the multiple-message approach of the army's socialization of soldiers and the practices that the institution has devised to constitute the socialization.

Wiseman then introduces us to the first subplot character, Hickman. Hickman is having trouble learning how to march, and he is getting "special training." He is hassled interminably, while in back of him a photographer takes a group photo, getting the soldiers to smile by having them say "whiskey" and "I like the army." This training sequence continues with bayonet training (special formations and some demonstrations) and is polished off by cudgel fighting, where a white man and a black man keep fighting after the drill is supposed to stop.

Here we begin a sequence on deviance and control. The black man is given a fine and seven days in correctional custody for fighting (bringing back memories of the famous "no fighting in the war room" line from *Dr. Strangelove*). He is lectured about "doing what you're told" and is informed that there is "no reason" for his fighting. Then Hickman is back again getting special help in lacing his boots. The sergeant who helps him then calls the chaplain and says that Hickman is suicidal. Hickman sees the chaplain, says that the guys are bugging him because they think he is messing up the company, and learns that he doesn't sound like someone really trying to get to the top. Deviance leads to control, either physical coercion or a redefinition of the situation that calls for new behavior. In a cut, we turn to the good soldiers that are being created, fighting with either great seriousness or joy, doing rigorous physical exercise and relaxing and talking about women. This sequence ends with a man being disciplined for bringing a soda and a magazine to the rifle range. The soldiers look like boy scouts, good kids, who are well behaved most of the time but occasionally silly, and above all who are naively enjoying what they are doing.

Until this point, the film has shown only the more obvious sociological and superficial views of the men involved in the process. We have hints of what it feels like to be a Hickman, but while he is probably typical of some recruits he seems so different from the rest of his cohort that we as an audience do not know who the majority of participants are. Then we see a sergeant talking about his religious thoughts, in this case someone else's Karma theory. He entertains some of the guys by saying that in reincarnation they might come back as either a black or a girl. Ways of determining sexual and personal identity within the culture are teased by this argument. This same theme is raised in the marching song that follows, describing a woman with a soldier's child. We then meet a soldier's parents who voice a similar insecurity about their son's sexual and personal growth. They are awed by his gun, almost afraid of him, telling him that he's going to get better at using it—he has to—that he is going to become a man—he has to—and that he should learn to be a true soldier, "a true American soldier."

Identity Problems

We then see a soldier who rejects the army and has resisted its indoctrination. He wants a court-martial, cares little about its consequences for his career and says that this is not his country. To his brother he adds that no one will change him (give him a new identity). He is followed in this sequence by a white soldier who is promoted, given "a niche in the world," as his mother calls it. The emotional and behavioral contrasts, the obvious reasons for them, the importance of family and self-participation in the socialization process and the rewards shown for participation all give the audience a rough social psychology by which to understand the institution's effectiveness and its limits.

These first sequences of the film set up the structure that the audience must know to understand the training process. The outline of the variables is complete, and the structure of the film is established. The rest of the film outlines the training process, its components and the final exam. This last part also deserves detailed analysis in order to cover the sociological points of interest.

Like the rest of the film, it begins with marching and a song, "Mr. Nixon, drop the bomb. I don't want to go to Nam." And the recruits start their Vietnam training in a jungle village set up by the army. In

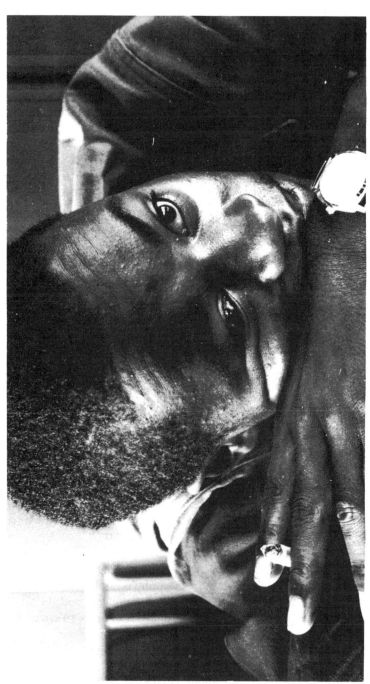

Wiseman's Basic Training *is a trip into the esthetics of socialization. It is a study of that part of the army that recruits and trains its novices, but more than that it is about a dance (or more superficially a game) that the army has developed to teach and ready their future participants for a position within that institution's structure.*

camouflage the soldiers demonstrate their discipline and fine training. Practicing their fighting procedures while guns fire BBs over them, they learn to run through fire, and they end up doing a search-and-destroy mission in a make-believe Vietnamese village. They are boy scouts on a camping trip, students taking an exam and soldiers all at the same time. They giggle when they find each other in the village, but in spite of the unreal quality of the exercise, as Wiseman says, they are also now capable of acting and in fact acting like trained hunters.

With a swing of the camera we see a long parade of newly trained soldiers marching into commencement. The "best soldier of basic training" receives a medal, the American Spirit of Honor Award, and proceeds to display the spirit of honor by reciting army history, telling his fellow soldiers to keep up the good fight and asking the Lord to give them the strength to keep on fighting. The film ends in marching.

Wiseman has brought the audience through basic training, looking at it from a social-psychological viewpoint, showing the detail and its meaning. The training has kept the game or dance quality throughout, and it has produced champions of the game, superb dancers ready to get into the big time that they have heard so much about.

Symbolic Rewards

Wiseman argues that institutions, in order to maintain themselves, require and maintain routines. In order to do easy time while being processed through the institutions, individuals conform to these routines. But to make the time really easy, they must also believe in what they are doing. They are superficially given institutional ideology to guide belief, but it is so confused or piecemeal that belief is often cut down to faith either in the institution's definition of itself as good or as necessary for survival. Those who cannot or do not develop this faith cannot make it in the institution. Some individuals receive the institution's symbolic messages of rewards and want to fit in. To do so they must strip themselves of any desire for logical and consistent meaning and instead perfect their faith and obedience in order to survive the structure and get the rewards. Actually, surviving the institution is problematic and the rewards, when spelled out, are not achieved by faith. But Wiseman shows that the structure, requiring faith in the institution rather than reasonable commitment, prevents its participants from questioning what they are doing.

My analysis to this point may have convinced the reader that Wiseman has always wanted to be a sociologist and finally got his chance. Nothing could be farther from the truth. His interests (outside of film) lie closer to literature; he sees in social life surreal qualities that he tries to convey in his films. This side of his work is less concerned with the methods of social science. In editing, Wiseman builds up a sense of the madness of institutional life, placing bits of misunderstandings on top of confused ideology on top of the complex of activities in all institutions on top of more and more participants in the institutions. By examining how he makes his films, we can begin to see how he builds the madness.

Film-making Style

Film-shooting styles determine what visual material is available for a final film. Wiseman's film-making style creates a sense of newness in the institutions he films. He does no preliminary research on the institutions he intends to film. In the process of getting money for the film, he writes a treatment (a brief outline of what the film is to be about) based on his understanding of the institution and uses this to guide his selection of images during shooting. Then in production Wiseman records his encounters with the institution. Thus, while his ignorance of the institutions he shoots might prevent him from choosing the most representative footage, in their raw form his recordings represent his personal education about an institution. Wiseman's films become polished visions of this learning/disenchantment/understanding process that those entering an institution go through before knowing their way around. The early stages of this process in turn comprise the madness of social life that Wiseman wants to convey.

Film Thought

Making sense out of footage is a film problem as well as an intellectual one, and Wiseman has developed characteristic film devices to build up both the meaning and the chaos of what he sees. He uses subplots or minibiographies, following specific individuals through a number of contacts with the institution; for example, a girl who has flunked a course in high school and her parents, or a man in the hospital who wants to leave against doctor's orders. These individuals are defined as deviant by the institution yet each sees his or her position as tenable. Filmically, these stories are threads of meaning, a picture of individuals caught between two definitions of a situation, a situation that the institution nominally has the power to define. In recording these sequences, Wiseman makes both an organizational and content decision to bound the meaning of the films by showing the boundaries of institutionally condoned behavior.

Inside these boundaries Wiseman places mirror-ball sequences—

groups of shots from all faces of the institution, each representing an aspect of institutional life. These sequences are related by containing parts of the subplots within them and/or footage from similar or common events, yet they are discrete images of information, each jumping out from the last. The films are built out of these sequences and subplots, the basic relationships between them finally being spelled out in a summary speech or its equivalent, declaring the need for faith in the institution.

Again the film-making style creates a logic and a limit to what is expressed. Each sequence examines some aspect of the institution's processes by the juxtaposition of examples. In *Hospital* Wiseman shows in one sequence: police discussing the frequent rejection of the elderly poor by hospital emergency rooms and the hours they spend in ambulances going from one hospital to the next, the emergency care of an elderly cardiac patient and gathering his history from a suspicious relative. Intellectually this sequence deals with the relationship between medical problems, ethnic or economic status and time in emergency-room care. Filmically, it is a choreography of emergency care—its rhythm and area for improvisation.

The subplots in these sequences add a nightmarish quality to the film, as an institution's rigidity seems to destroy its purpose when individuals act inappropriately. The fate of the cardiac patient in the example above makes up one of the subplots in *Hospital*. The patient's emergency care is followed by a relative being interviewed by the doctor from the emergency room. The relative is reluctant to give information to the doctor because she thinks he is accusing her of neglect. The viewer, having seen that the cardiac patient is almost lifeless, experiences the wait for information as interminable. The film makes the audience both examine and feel the potentially fatal procedural and personal impact of organizational problems.

One of the values of Wiseman's interest in surrealism is that he points out the different levels on which institutional processing is defined and where some of these definitions conflict.

On one level he shows that institutions are places that define behavior ideologically. Individuals are caught in ideological binds unless or until they can define themselves in institutional terms. Since the ideologies in most institutions are confused, it is difficult for many people to see how they can define themselves in such terms. Frequently, there are class differences in both knowing appropriate ideologies and accepting them. But for those who cannot accept institutions' definitions of themselves but still want their services, the institutions create personal dissonance. To successfully deny the institution's definitions and ideology, individuals must deny their need for them. For instance, one man leaves the hospital against his doctor's orders. He feels free to do this because he says he can take medicine outside the institution. He defines the medicine rather than the institution as the source of health. On the other hand, an old woman with diabetes who spends most of her money on hospital care thanks the nurse when she pays her bill because she needs the hospital. She feels that the hospital maintains her health and is glad to follow its rules of payment. These two individuals relate differently to the institution's definition of itself as a place of healing.

Particularly in *High School* and *Basic Training* Wiseman shows the institutions primarily as indoctrination centers. In these he illustrates the contradictions, insincerity and even emptiness of ideology; he also shows its effectiveness. The girls in *High School* learn how to walk and to compare their bodies to a form or ideal of feminine beauty. They all fall short of the form. One girl, who wears a short dress to the prom, learns that she will destroy the situation by her attire, as though the institution would give her the freedom to do so. In *Titticut Follies,* an inmate at Bridgewater gets a shave and the guards joke with him, but their jokes convey their antipathy towards him. There is something ideological that novices to the institutions must learn in order to get along, but there are frequently contradictory or missing elements in the lessons.

In *Law and Order* and *Hospital* the distance between ideology and practice in institutions is illustrated repeatedly. While this is nothing new to most people, Wiseman's presentation of this distance is exciting because the ideologies are shown as confused. What is practiced is related to an ideal or truth that is never clearly articulated. Given the inconsistencies of institutional ideology, the adoption of informal procedural rules makes sense. The police explain to a prostitute that being arrested is part of her role, and to play it she must learn not to resist arrest. For men who have learned that they must arrest lawbreakers, this practice makes absolute sense; it makes their job easier. A female doctor in *Hospital* tells a man who thinks he has syphilis that he must not be ashamed of himself, and anyway they are not sure that is what he has. He doesn't understand (we would suspect) that shame must hinge on diagnosis. She on the other hand, does not understand that a medical problem might not be simply a medical problem to a patient, that to say (as she should) that he should not be ashamed does not remove the issue of shame from medical practice.

With these two institutional foci we see Wiseman presenting a particular model of institutions. He shows us individuals acting within unclear and often bypassed constraints. He shows us the individual and the institution in the misunderstandings and the imperfect definitions of people that characterize institutional interaction.

On top of this, we do not follow single individuals through the films, but rather constantly see new faces—individuals beginning to encounter the institution we are learning more and more about. As we see each new sequence, the multitudes pouring through our experience and the obstacles people run into because they are novices, the madness of the institutions seems to grow. The novices appear afraid and confused, while those running the institutions seem tired and frustrated, both groups often being unaware of what they are doing to others and to themselves. It seems in these films that the consequence of building institutions on faith is that they become populated with socially blind people.

Frederick Wiseman attracts audiences because he builds exciting images of interesting institutions. He holds the viewer's attention because the content of the images is as complex as the subject. But what is most impressive about his films is their many levels of meaning—the visual metaphors that both his films and the institutions he shoots are built on. Audiences from the institutions, though they are blinded by faith, like Wiseman's films on first showing; he does not construct an ideology counter to their own. But once his films are reviewed, institutional personnel start their lawsuits. They discover that Wiseman, as film-maker has drawn audiences to look at his films and, while they watch, teaches them a new way to see social institutions.

Sputtering Fires of Black Revolution: *BURN!*

Richard E. Rubenstein

This is less a movie review than a postmortem. Several months after its initial run *BURN!* appears to have burnt out—despite the potent combination of Gillo Pontecorvo's direction, Marlon Brando's acting and United Artists' distribution network. According to *Chicago Sun-Times* movie critic, Roger Ebert, the film's short run is attributable to cost overruns and a weak audience response. More conspiracy-minded movie fans may wish to speculate further, considering that *BURN!* is a very exciting piece of revolutionary propaganda, that United Artists Corporation, the company that gave the world James Bond, is controlled by Democratic bigwigs Robert P. Benjamin and Arthur F. Krim, and that the same company has also managed to avoid releasing *The Battle of Algiers* to neighborhood theaters. I saw *BURN!* in one of the "black" theaters in Chicago's Loop, and can report that its message was not lost on the large audience, which greeted Brando's assassination at the end of the film with cries of "Right on!"

BURN! is a distinguished failure, nominally starring Marlon Brando as the nineteenth-century C.I.A.-Special Adviser type, but really starring director Pontecorvo as a victim of Hollywood film-making. Brando, British agent and soldier of fortune, is on screen for at least sixty minutes in several incarnations. Slick, tough and worldly, Brando is the classic outside agitator. He foments rebellion among the rural blacks of a Caribbean island against their Portuguese colonial masters and convinces the local white settler bourgeoisie to declare independence in order to break free of Portuguese trade restrictions. In a memorable climax to this first act (even the film's format is theatrical), Brando confronts the black leader, who has entered the capital in an attempt to carry the revolution through, and forces him to admit his incapacity to rule. The scene ends with the ragtag people's army stacking its weapons obediently in the city

BURN! *is the equivalent, on film, of an illuminated Marxist-Leninist handbook,*
"Pontecorvo's Illustrated Guide to Third World Struggle." Successive segments of
the film correspond to the Marxian stages of political development . . . ."

square. (The black audience at the Woods Theater didn't like this a bit.
They know all about gun control.)

In Act Two, Brando returns to the island as agent for a British super-
company to find that the comprador bourgeoisie has by now lost its illusory autonomy to his employer. The company has, in fact, provoked a
primitive proletarian revolt by squeezing the black peasantry too hard.
The whites are weak, ineffectual, riven by liberal principles. Brando
therefore engineers the assassination of the liberal leader, replaces him
with a compliant military tool and masterminds a ghastly counterinsur-
gency campaign against the rebels. No longer a gay adventurer, Brando
is now the bitter realist, the technocrat par excellence, manfully thinking
about the unthinkable and practising it. The Indochina allegory is unmis-
takable. Without political restraint, Brando succeeds in the nineteenth-
century equivalent of "bombing them back into the Stone Age," captur-
ing the rebel leader in the bargain (groans from the audience).

Coda: In order to avoid making a martyr, Brando offers the black
leader freedom, thinking to have him disposed of quietly while trying to
escape (the Lumumba deal, essentially). The leader knowingly declines.

Brando, who has not enjoyed the genocide any more than, say, Henry Kissinger, then has a *crise de conscience;* he makes a genuine offer of freedom, which is also declined. The leader is hanged. While walking across a dock to his ship, amidst a sea of hostile black faces, Brando is anonymously stabbed to death. Drums in the background, crescendo (Right on!).

Since this film is really a sequel to *The Battle of Algiers,* a comparision is instructive. The latter employed the rough, grainy style of the newsreel and an anonymous cast; *BURN!* is a slick technicolor historical spectacular dominated by a single star. The subject of *The Battle of Algiers* was a specific, real battle (in immediate terms, a losing one) within the larger continuum of the Algerian Revolution; *BURN!*'s subject is a fictionalized revolt on a mythical isle. In *The Battle of Algiers,* cinéma vérité techniques (including the use of actual combatants as actors) subordinated ideology to drama; the film's messages about the nature of revolutionary warfare seemed to emerge from the action itself rather than from the director's brain. *BURN!* is the equivalent, on film, of an illuminated Marxist-Leninist handbook, "Pontecorvo's Illustrated Guide to Third World Struggle." Successive segments of the film correspond to the Marxian stages of political development and we recognize, like old friends appearing in drag, Marx's critique of bourgeois democracy, Lenin's theory of imperialism as the last stage of capitalism, Mao's emphasis on the struggle between good country and bad city, Fanon's identification of colonial liberation with racial liberation. Unwittingly, the movie illustrates another notion of Mao's—the idea that it is impossible to produce revolutionary art which is not good art.

Viewing the film, first, simply as a Marxist-Leninist morality play, one notices a conspicuous absence: the triumph of the revolution is not portrayed. (Interestingly, it is portrayed in *The Battle of Algiers,* but almost as an afterthought.) This is a profoundly pessimistic work, or (which is the same thing) a work of chiliastic optimism. Despite the obvious parallels between *BURN!*'s revolution and the Indochinese, in *BURN!* the spirit of the people does not prove stronger than the Man's technology. Brando is the Man (the Star); he dominates the picture totally; his murder in the end by an anonymous representative of the people suggests the inevitability of the final revolution in the same way that the damnation of Faust suggests the final triumph of God: the Fausts and Kissingers of the world will get theirs eventually, but meanwhile. . . . The faith in revolutionary triumph which Pontecorvo professes here is precisely that—faith—and it is by no means clear how that faith is to be realized. One could, perhaps, say in extenuation that *BURN!* portrays a primitive rebellion, not a modern revolution, and that the spirit of primitive

There is a mysticism about the masses here which is fundamentally at variance with the Marxian insight that it is people—real men and women—who make history. One is compelled to ask when and how these dumb brutes will develop the consciousness which a class may have "for itself," as Marx says, and not just "of itself"?

rebellion, like that of the film, is romantic, heroic, nationalistic, chiliastic, doomed. As Eqbal Ahmed has pointed out to me, Pontecorvo is too ambitious to produce a dramatic version of, say, the Indian Mutiny. He wants the film to be "relevant" to contemporary revolutionary struggles—to be a message movie. The effect is wildly anachronistic, with Brando (William Westmoreland in knickers) the wildest anachronism of them all.

Corrupting Techniques

What has gone wrong here? *The Battle of Algiers* had been criticized, despite its great art, for yielding to commercialism in overemphasizing the spectacular, military-organization aspects of the battle and the role of heroic leadership, when what we needed (need) to know was what sort of mundane political work bound both revolutionary leaders and cadres so closely to the people. *BURN!*, even more commercial in its appeal, raises the issue more poignantly. Perhaps Pontecorvo felt that he could use Hollywood techniques to help undermine the Empire which gave them birth. The opposite seems to have occurred: that is, the techniques have corrupted the message. For example, the blacks in the film ("the people") are not its motive force, or history's; they are extras in every sense of the word. They do not revolt—they are stirred to revolt by the white outside agitator. They are not individuals, but a formless, basically incomprehensible mass led by a cardboard figure of a leader. There is a mysticism about the masses here which is fundamentally at variance with the Marxian insight that it is people—real men and women—who make history. One is compelled to ask when and how these dumb brutes will develop the consciousness which a class may have "for itself," as Marx says, and not just "of itself." Someday, somehow. But where will this consciousness come from? We are not told. Perhaps, through the leader sacrificing himself at the scaffold.

Clearly, this is a Hollywood vision, juxtaposing crowds of undifferentiated extras with an elite of stars. It is also a Christian vision (the two are not unrelated) with the rebel leader as Lamb of God and Brando as Antichrist. Ironically, Brando, star of the film, ends by becoming the star of its ideology—the Lucifer of this *Paradise Lost*. He is the only personality in the movie, the only force comprehensible in human terms. When he unleashes terror upon the black population of the island, when he isolates the rebels and drives them into a lonely trap, when he plots the leader's murder and then offers him freedom, we understand exactly why he acts as he does. He is one of us, a man, although an evil man. But we do not understand who these drumbeating rebels are or how they have become isolated from their people—or why, unlike the Vietnamese, they are so easily defeated by sheer force. For this reason, revolution—the heart of Marxian thought—remains a mystery in *BURN!*, a primal catastrophe postdated well into the future, more akin to the Biblical apocalypse than to the process in which men now alive participate, or hope to participate.

I am driven to conclude that it is simply not possible to make a revolutionary movie which is consistent with the accepted dramatic values of commercial movie-making. Godard, among others, recognizes this, although whether or not his art represents an advance over that of Pontecorvo is an open question. In any event, see *BURN!* (if you can find it). See it, and reflect that people are not redeemed through the sacrifice of martyrs. They redeem themselves through their own struggle. Political consciousness is not bestowed upon them like the grace of God. Ordinary folk raise their own consciousness, painfully and against great odds, because it is their nature to attempt to realize their humanity, to seek understanding, and to help each other.

The Discreet Charm of the Bourgeoisie

Irving Louis Horowitz

The Discreet Charm of the Bourgeoisie might be called a continental version of *Dinner at Eight,* forty years later. The difference is that the nouveaux riches are no longer nouveaux, but have learned to live within their means and have lost their moral sense in the process. Both films are organized by the dining room. *Dinner at Eight* is concerned with everything that happens before the eating begins, a last fling before the Great Depression impinges its ugly truths on the lives of a still confident middle class. In *The Discreet Charm of the Bourgeoisie,* worries of economic depression have long since yielded to concerns about political revolution, although such concerns are expressed only in nightmares and fantasies. *The Discreet Charm* is, from beginning to end, a dining room farce; every "action" scene takes place around eating. In this way, Luis Buñuel leads us to see the difference between affluence and opulence, wealth and waste.

Buñuel has employed the device of the collective eating scene before. In both *The Exterminating Angel* and *Viridiana,* dining is employed surrealistically, to show the depravity of people by comparing them to the beasts from which Darwin elevated them. In these films, Buñuel's eating scenes tended to be of Hogarthian proportions—ribald as well as revolting. But in *The Discreet Charm,* depravity is given a specific class character: manners intersect with eating to produce a shadow of civility while disguising the absence of its substance. Here the joys of the feast are punctuated by a comedy of errors: missed cues, coming to eat at an associate's house on the wrong day, going to a restaurant and finding a funeral, and experiencing sexual desire at a socially embarrassing moment. But in the end, Hogarth is displaced by Mao. The feast is disrupted by the slaughter of the meat eaters.

From García Lorca's *Blood Wedding* to Carlos Fuentes' *Aura,* modern Spanish and Latin American literature has echoed the theme of death as the expiation of private and social guilt. The search for sensual pleasure, while inevitable, is countered by the resolution that only death can bring. The old gardener who had poisoned the bishop's parents is given absolution and the final rites of the Church by the bishop—after which he murders him, despite the fact that the gardener is about to die a natural death. This is necessary, not because the bishop is depraved or seeks revenge, but rather because a violent death is just. No matter what consolations the last rites of the Church may provide in the next world, the biblical laws of this world must be met. And so, every death, real or illusory, factual or fantasized, must be violent to the degree that people in the natural world have sinned.

It is no wonder that Buñuel has an ambiguous relationship to Christianity here as in every other one of his films. The hypocrisy of the Church, the wickedness of its excesses, the vanities of its ecclesiastical leaders, are again apparent; but here, Buñuel has made peace with his own deep religiosity, his own beliefs in a just and good Providence. The bishop, for all his vanity, is strangely human; he desires a pastoral life and takes joy in wearing the clothing of a gardener and using the sickle of the toiler. "You have heard of the worker-priest movement," he says in seeking the gardener's job from the incredulous bourgeois family. "Well, I represent the worker-bishop movement." The bishop-turned-gardener still seeks the reward of his ecclesiastical position—deference from others—but he is happier with the inner rewards of returning to the land toiled by his parents. Buñuel does not reconcile his attitudes toward Christianity in this movie because such a pretentious and preposterous aim is not intended. Instead, the agony of the two faces of the Church: opulence and poverty, devotion and defiance, is revealed with a greater sense of compassion and less tendentiousness than in Buñuel's previous films. If Spain under Franco has not yet made its peace with Buñuel, the exiled genius has at least made his peace with Spain under God.

The French critic André Breton has noted in Durkheim-like fashion, that "what is most remarkable about the fantastic is that the fantastic does not exist. Everything is real." Buñuel, true to his earlier work in *Un chien andalou* and *L'age d'or,* has a few surrealistic pigeons up his sleeve in *The Discreet Charm.* A coffee shop claims to be out of coffee and tea (but does have water). A restaurant conducts a funeral for a deceased owner (but food is being served). At parties, generals pass marijuana to colonels (while ambassadorial drug dealers pontificate over the evils of pot and how it leads to higher evils). A married couple leaves guests waiting downstairs because of a passionate need to fornicate (in their own garden). Couples come to supper on the wrong evening (matching

In The Discreet Charm, *depravity is given a specific class character: manners intersect with eating to produce a shadow of civility while disguising the absence of its substance. Here the joys of the feast are punctuated by a comedy of errors . . . . But in the end, Hogarth is replaced by Mao. The feast is disrupted by the slaughter of the meat eaters.*

army maneuvers in the French countryside taking place on the wrong day).

What is special about surrealism in the seventies is its subtlety. No longer are temporal and causal time reversals done primarily for shock value. Rather, they illustrate the pretentiousness of bourgeois discretion;

the impossibility of reconciling every trifling incongruity into a polite middle-class framework, and the need to try. Here too art and criticism intersect with more telling effect than in previous films. A foremost member of the Spanish "generation of 27" has evolved into a "revolutionist of 72."

Buñuel has produced a masterpiece in film making, the crowning achievement in a career of continuous film innovation. But as in so many of his other films, the tension between artistic entertainment and social energy remains intact. This is exemplified in the dream sequences in which neo-Freudian Oedipal complexes compete with neo-Marxian social messages for attention: the young military officer poisons his father on instructions from his mother (who has been dead six years) after she tells him that his real father (shown in spattered blood) was killed by the imposter father; the prison chief inspector dreams of a police officer who, doing penitence for having been cruel and heartless to young prisoners, returns each July fourteenth (again, spattered with blood) to open the jails in expiation of his crimes. In a final dream, the Ambassador of Miranda (played brilliantly by Fernando Rey) highlights the theme of revenge and death, as bloody carcasses are strewn about in demonstration of the violent end to meaningless lives.

This ambiguity can be understood, if not entirely resolved, by appreciation that this is a Spanish film made in the French language. Its passions and emotions are derived from the soil of Spain, not the more delicately laced French tradition of cinema verité as exemplified by Jean Renoir's *Rules of the Game* (with which *The Discreet Charm* invites comparison). Lorca-like themes of repressed love, maternal domination, justice as expressed through violent death, are all symbolized by the constancy of bloodletting (even one of the dream victims of death through poisoning is seen bloodied about the mouth). This evokes the angular violence of Spanish interpersonal history, which more than anywhere else in Europe, was carried over into its political structure. Buñuel's skill is in relieving the tension by having the storytellers react normally to their dreams. Waking up in a cold sweat and downing food becomes a test of being alive. The general relief felt when finding oneself alive and out of the dream world is expressed by a return to bestiality rather than an elevation in humanity.

The dream sequences are of two types: those recited ritualistically by the teller before an audience, in which the teller receives relief and absolution in a thoroughly psychoanalytic manner; and dreams actually experienced and portrayed, not as exhibitionistic releases from tension, but as expressions of that tension. In these latter dreams, social values are most directly expressed as the thoroughgoing frustrations of the police lieutenant with the contradictions of a job that ostensibly ensures law and order, but does so through such lawless devices as torture and castration of political prisoners. The quintessential dream of the ambassador, which in effect is the nightmare of the bourgeoisie itself, is to be brought face to face with reality by being brought to the edge of death by guerrillas and revolutionists who do not understand the limits of bourgeois civility.

The final dream sequence is organically linked to the final eating sequence to form a Gotterdammerung of meaning in death. Political reality and social consciousness impinge on the bourgeois representatives only as a result of fear of violence, that form of seemingly spontaneous violence that can take place at any time and under any circumstances because it is outside the law, outside the norms of polite society. Were it not for such lawlessness, nothing could awaken the bourgeoisie from its torpor. Buñuel is quite clear on this point: the barrel of the gun, not reason, is the source of consciousness—for victim and the victimizer alike. But even here, Buñuel adds a distinctive touch: a brilliant dialogue between the ambassador and a guerrilla girl *cum* assassin who is caught by the ambassador. Their conversation is punctuated by the ambassador's effete wave of a handkerchief, signalling that his guards should remove the guerrilla girl and do away with her. So even at the most intimate level, the bourgeoisie is incapable of doing its own killing without the aid of hired assassins. Buñuel's distinction between those who kill for principle and those who buy protection to defend privilege is quite strong. Again, this is a thoroughly Spanish aspect of the film scenario.

The organization of the film into eight eating-dining segments is a brilliant device for moving the viewer from scene to scene with continuity. It also expresses the simple truth that so much of all life, not only bourgeois life, is organized by pedestrian activity. But the film does much more than that: it shows how the bourgeoisie takes questions of eating and drinking (how to prepare a martini, in what sort of glass, and at what speed to drink it) as the essence of life itself. Good housekeeping relates not just to their life-style, but permeates the substance of their existence. Table conversation is taken up with matters of food, and when it drifts from this omnipotent subject it either leads to astrological banalities of a most hilarious nature or to discussions of certain minor embarrassments that occur in Miranda (hunger, torture, harboring Nazi war criminals) which call forth even more incredible banalities ("One should not exaggerate the number of Nazis in Miranda, they are to be found everywhere . . . . I have spoken to the Nazi you mention, the word butcher is far too strong, he is a quite civilized sort.") In effect, politics itself is bad man-

The organization of the film into eight eating-dining segments is a brilliant device for moving the viewer from scene to scene with continuity. It also expresses the simple truth that so much of all life, not only bourgeois life, is organized by pedestrian activity.

ners. Reality at the dinner table is in poor taste. And that, after all, is what the discreet charm of the bourgeoisie is all about.

The film takes place in a political vacuum; we are in the midst of the private lives of a diplomat and his entourage. The one thing the diplomat seems incapable of rendering is a political judgment or a sober thought on worldly affairs. Even in describing his own country, he can only sound like he is conducting a travelogue. His nation becomes some sort of grotesque admixture of Argentina, Uruguay and Chile, called Miranda —simply a delightful place for his business associate (the business is heroin traffic) to visit. The word bourgeoisie is thus linked to business and commerce as well as manners and mores—the huge, illegal traffic-king in heroin, under the cloak of diplomatic immunity, underwrites the entrepreneurial spirit of three families of friends, lovers, pushers and dipsomaniacs. The wonderful thing is that Buñuel is able to make all of these strange goings-on happen in a value-neutral, morally irrelevant context.

The shocking coming to true consciousness for the bourgeoisie is the scene towards the end of the film where the diplomat dreams of his din-ner being invaded by guerrillas who, in revenge for a quite real hygienic murder of a would-be female assassin, wipe out the dinner guests in a bloodbath—while the diplomat hero hides under the table from where he attempts to sneak his unfinished dinner. He awakens from the nightmare as the guerrillas take aim at him. In a scene reminiscent of *The Loved One*, the ambassador is caught in the act of raiding the refrigerator just after the dreamed blood bath.

The "message" sometimes obscured by the levity of the dinner pro-ceedings, is nonetheless permitted to surface in key dialogues between the young female guerrilla and the old diplomat. For only when he is con-fronted by the force of weapons or better, by the threat of annihilation, does reality intrude upon the discreet charms of the bourgeoisie. There is no responsiveness to the sufferings of the poor, no sensitivity to the needs of this quasi-mythic Latin American country he presumably serves. The purpose of guerrillas in the film, and no doubt for Buñuel in reality, is to bring some sort of reality to bear on the culinary proceed-ings. Without the guerrillas, the life of the diplomatic corps would be simply a round of parties and dining engagements. It is precisely this goal that the guerrillas frustrate in reality and in the dream sequences. The bourgeoisie lack a consciousness, but retain a capacity to react to the destructive aims of their adversaries. They do not think through causative sequences, but try to rid themselves of nuisances which would disturb the delicately woven patterns of self-deception that substitutes manners for morals and elevates style to substance.

One serious problem with *The Discreet Charm* is whether the portrayal is typical or stereotypical—a true representation of the bourgeois cum diplomat or a false representation based on a radical chic of a deracinated European consciousness. This is not an unimportant distinction, since so much hinges upon the accuracy of the portrayal. And it is at this point that the plot of this plotless film dissolves. Is the diplomatic corps, above the third attaché level at least, composed simply of swindlers, gourmets and transparent fools? I suspect not. Indeed, the time has long since passed when diplomacy was organically linked to the manners of the European bourgeoisie. Diplomacy has become mechanized, coldly efficient, part of the scientific determination of national interests in a war gaming universe. Ironically, the diplomatic corps like its bureaucratic counterparts elsewhere remains strangely indifferent to real politics, very much linked to a hygienic view of national realities and moral imperatives.

Buñuel's genius as expressed in *The Discreet Charm* is something of a period piece, more a reflection of a time of his youth rather than the present universe of nuclear fear and trembling. Latin America is simply no longer a place of reactionary banana republics harboring fugitives and fascists from justice; nor are its embassies passive recipients of the glories of French cuisine. It is not that Buñuel is unaware of such changes, but that he seems unsure how to give such change expression. The coldly mechanical and methodical bureaucratic reality of the bourgeoisie (certainly the diplomatic variety) is only partially captured by Buñuel. In this respect, the film should be judged for its metaphorical aims rather than empirical terms. Luis Buñuel himself would probably rest content with that.

Amarcord

Michael A. Ledeen

In the dialect of the Romagna, the province and dialect of Federico Fellini's childhood, *Amarcord* means "Ah, I remember" (drawn from the Italian, *Ah, mi ricordo*). When asked about his selection of the title by an Italian weekly several months before the film's release, Fellini said that while everyone knew the film represented a sort of autobiography, they had overlooked one of the most important facets of the title: the word itself and the mysteriousness that it evokes. The sound of the word suggests the nature of the epoch from which it comes: soft, melancholy, strange. This, he said, was the essence of life during the early thirties in Italy.

He had chosen his title as carefully as his characters, his music, and his fantasies. When Fellini makes a film, he first outlines the scenes he wants to shoot and then literally draws the characters he wants to put in them. He thus starts with a list of actions to be filmed and a set of drawings for the casting department. Having determined these elements, he then sets out to find faces that correspond to his drawings, hoping to find people (actors or not) who are capable of interpreting the role he has assigned to their faces. The result is an almost unbelievable assortment of faces and bodies that have undergone a transformation under the creative process of his direction.

Fellini has outdone himself in *Amarcord*. His actors are utterly striking: there is, for example, the tall, gawky mental case who emerges from the asylum once a month, the proprietress of the town tobacco store endowed with breasts big enough to smother a man (the incarnation of Fellini's most common sexual fantasy), the Fascist leaders who seem to have sprung to life from the cartoons of the period, the hard-working, frustrated father with a large cyst on his bald head, the town beauty with a rear like a soft, round pillow (the role was supposed to have been

When Fellini makes a film, he first outlines the scenes he wants to shoot and then literally draws the characters he wants to put in them. He thus starts with a list of actions to be filmed and a set of drawings for the casting department. Having determined these elements, he then sets out to find faces that correspond to his drawings, hoping to find people (actors or not) who are capable of interpreting the role he has assigned to their faces.

played by Sandra Millo, but she was not available). The film is a gallery of unforgettable caricatures.

Along with this brilliant job of casting, Fellini's choice of music borders on the miraculous. As always, there are the circus themes, used to punctuate the theatrical and comic aspects of life in Italy, the clownishness of small people trying to act like great men. But there are other marvelous touches: "Stormy Weather" floating through the window of the petit-bourgeois kitchen while husband and wife engage in a hilarious melodramatic argument about eating, and other themes from the thirties in the background when people try to act as if they were acting in movies from the period.

None of this will be news to those who are familiar with Fellini's work. Like all his other movies, this one mixes fantasy and reality together pell-mell, so that one is frequently uncertain whether any given scene actually took place or whether it is composed of Fellini's recollections of his dreams. This is quite appropriate to the subject matter of the film, for the fantasies of the thirties were every bit as important as the reality of the epoch. This brings us to the core of *Amarcord,* for however elegant the techniques of the director may be, Fellini has also focused on an extremely important and controversial theme.

It is important to remember that *Amarcord* was produced during a very significant period in the history of Italian cinema. More precisely, it was done at the end of years of work by Italian directors on explicitly political and recent historical subjects: *The Conformist, Sacco and Vanzetti, The Spider's Strategem, The Garden of the Finzi-Continis, Tales of Love and Anarchy, The Damned.* These films were produced with an explicitly political purpose: to create an anti-Fascist awareness in the minds of the audience. For the most part, these anti-Fascist movies were produced by directors with chicly leftist ideals (Bertolucci is perhaps the most notorious of these), and they tended to portray fascism as something monstrous, something grotesque, something utterly decadent and bizarre. Fellini's achievement in *Amarcord* was to present a genuine document of the Fascist period, largely free of the polemical quality that characterized most of the other films of this genre and artistically far superior to them. Finally a film director has succeeded in telling us what life under Italian fascism was like.

In *Amarcord,* fascism is of a piece with both the life of the town and the countryside, penetrating all aspects of existence. The symbol that Fellini uses for this penetration is one of those the Fascists used themselves: a figure on a motorcycle, who appears several times in the film to disrupt a traditional ceremony or to break a serene mood. Thus the mechanized, speedy, and noisy machine disrupts the placid, traditional, and sleepy town in the Romagna. The sexual significance of the motorcycle is significant here as well, for the domination of the city by fascism is clearly conceived of in sexual terms.

Just as the motorcycle appeals above all to the young, so fascism becomes the depository of youthful fantasies. If the young boys fantasize the conquest of the beautiful Gradisca (the town beauty, whose name means "to receive with pleasure"), it is a Fascist officer who finally takes

Fellini's achievement in Amarcord *was to present a genuine document of the Fascist period, largely free of the polemical quality that characterized most of the other films of this genre and artistically far superior to them. Finally a film director has succeeded in telling us what life under Italian Fascism was like.*

her away; if the chubbiest kid in town is frustrated because he cannot get any attention from a pretty girl, fascism will set it right in his daydreams, when Mussolini orders the girl to marry him as a "hero of the Fascist Revolution."

The brilliance of fascism, if one can talk this way about something so odious, was to have understood the mentality of Italians in the twenties and thirties, and to have adapted its political necessities to the cultural and social realities of the Italian world. This world was characterized in

As we see in Amarcord, *the Fascists really represented the triumph of adolescent wish-fulfillment over the world of parents and teachers. Since Italian males often remain largely schoolboys at heart . . . a regime that exalted adolescent virtues was enormously popular.*

large part of generational conflict and, as we see in *Amarcord,* the Fascists really represented the triumph of adolescent wish-fulfillment over the world of parents and teachers. Since Italian males often remain largely schoolboys at heart (anyone who doubts this can take a long drive on an *autostrada* in bad weather or walk along an Italian beach in good weather), a regime that exalted adolescent virtues was enormously popular. To be sure, fascism's triumphs were fraudulent for the most part, and Fellini shows us this emptiness in a brilliant scene in which the Fascists ruthlessly gun down a phonograph that is playing a Socialist melody in the bell tower of the town's central piazza. When the machine falls, they burst into a militant fighting song and go for a drink.

The serious side of fascism, the infamous treatment of enemies with clubs and castor oil, is not seen publicly but performed in the darkness of night inside the offices of the *Questura.* We see a vaguely pseudo-Socialist housing contractor receive the castor oil "cure," and then, typically, when he staggers home and takes a bath, his son's reaction is to laugh at the smell of his father's clothes.

I do not want to give the impression that *Amarcord* is only about fascism; it is far more than that. There are other equally important themes in the film, most of which will be familiar by now to Fellini watchers. But I can not resist describing the scene that has stayed with me longest: when the insane son climbs to the top of a tree in the early afternoon and starts screaming at the top of his lungs, "I want a woman!" After an entire day of this, the family sends to the asylum for help, and who arrives? A midget nun (where does Fellini find these people?) whose face we never see, who briskly climbs the ladder to the tree and returns with the maniac in tow.

This is one of two clergy scenes and is, so to speak, the punch line of the first, which is the confessional of the schoolboys. The priest, typically distracted by the more important aspects of his office (the floral display around the altar), routinely asks them about honoring their parents, and then really digs in: "Do you play with yourself? Tell me. Of course you do. Do you know the Lord cries when you touch yourself? Tell me about it." Years later they end up in trees screaming for help.

Fellini tells us about the loneliness of those years, the emptiness of them, and the silliness that characterized the lives of those who underwent the Fascist experience. There is a magic moment when he answers Bertolucci in his own metaphor: a group of schoolboys peeks in the keyhole of the luxury hotel outside the town in the middle of the winter and as the soft music of their fantasies fills the air heavy with fog, each begins to dance with an imaginary partner, whirling and dipping to the fantastic music he hears in his head. Here there is none of the ribald decadence of *The Conformist* or *The Damned*. These young Fascists-to-be have no one to dance with except the women in their dreams.

On Lina Wertmuller

Joan Mellen

Acclaimed by many as the finest woman director working in movies today, Lina Wertmuller has recently come under serious attack by some women critics and viewers on feminist grounds. At first there had been demurs over Wertmuller's lingering wide-angle exposure of the fleshy, pitted posterior of the wife of a minor country official in *The Seduction of Mimi.* Whatever his faults, which included caving in to the Mafia, the hero Mimi was never caricatured for his rolls of flab. Mimi's faults revealed spiritual weakness; the woman was gross and Wertmuller seemed to be delighting in this grossness for its own sake. When Wertmuller admitted in an interview that she used *two* women for the scene, presumably because the buxom Elena Fiore was not fat enough, she added insult to injury.

It was also noted that whatever their strengths, the women in *Love and Anarchy,* which was released next in the United States, were all prostitutes. Wertmuller, then, was no better than the slew of male directors portraying women as either call girls or hapless domestics. That a talented woman director should continue to perpetuate old demeaning stereotypes was not to be forgiven.

But the outcry broke loose over Wertmuller's next three features which appeared in rapid succession: *Swept Away, All Screwed Up,* and *Seven Beauties* (the latter dubbed by one woman critic "Seven Fatties"). Viewing *Swept Away* literally, the feminists were especially incensed as Mariangela Melato thrilled before the abuse heaped upon her by Giancarlo Giannini. Wertmuller was called a male chauvinist for portraying a woman in masochistic enslavement to a man, for having her grovel at the feet of the contemptuous Sicilian servant with whom she is stranded on a desert island. For was not Wertmuller humiliating the woman merely to cram down our throats the spurious thesis that a working-class lover is so

Acclaimed by many as the finest woman director working in movies today, Lina Wertmuller has recently come under serious attack by some women critics and viewers on feminist grounds.

virile that we would at once be swept away by his abusive charms? Are we, in this day of a new women's consciousness, being treated to a refurbishing of the old myth that women secretly wish to be abused and in fact can attain sexual gratification only by submitting to violence and degradation? And this thesis from a woman who calls herself a revolutionary?

For these feminists Wertmuller could do nothing right after *Swept Away.* The women in *All Screwed Up,* made before *Swept Away,* were either whores or maids lusting after a life-style exactly like that of their rich employers and more than willing to sacrifice love for possessions. The men, it was pointed out, were the only people capable of love and devotion. And Wertmuller repeated the offense in *Seven Beauties* with her grotesque portrayal of the Nazi commandant (Shirley Stoler), a hideous woman in the role of dispenser of unspeakable cruelty. So anxious to demean women, went this reasoning, Wertmuller had to defy history; for how many women under Nazism, with its insistence upon *kirche, kinder,* and *kuche,* rose to so responsible a position? The hero Pasqualino's seven sisters, not to mention his beloved mother, become cheap whores with their black hair dyed blonde when the Americans occupy Italy after the war. Thus, the feminists conclude, Wertmuller the misogynist is at it again, bartering the dignity of women for a cheap, easy joke.

But are Wertmuller's women mere cows, anxious to be mastered and abused? Is she pandering to a current backlash against the struggle of women to be taken seriously? I think not. Nowhere in these attacks on Wertmuller is mentioned Fiore ("flower"), the strong noble woman (played by Mariangela Melato) at the center of *The Seduction of Mimi.* Although Mimi gives her the eye much in the manner that Pasqualino will the Nazi commandant, Fiore will sleep with him only if and when she truly loves him. As part of his seduction he calls her "comrade," appealing to her anarchist sympathies. Women may have always fallen for him, but Fiore has too much integrity. "Trotskyist doesn't mean whore," she says with dignity, a woman of principle unequalled by any of the male characters in any of Wertmuller's films.

Once she does fall in love with Mimi, Fiore demands his utter devotion, admitting no compromises. Mimi's equal in all ways and his superior in character, Fiore exerts so humanizing an influence on her callow lover that only when *she* responds can he make love to her. Fiore bears Mimi's child, photographed with her baby by Wertmuller as if she were a Madonna. She stands for the courage to struggle for freedom and decency, while Mimi slowly, through cowardice and self-absorption falls into the hands of the Mafia. And once his fall is conclusive, and he addresses his fellow Mafiosi as "cousins," she leaves him. At the end Fiore rides off with an old friend of Mimi's who had stuck by his beliefs despite hard times. For her to stay would be to acquiesce in his corruption. Although she loves him, she departs—leaving Mimi (as the camera and Wertmuller recede with her) a speck in the sand, mired in a wasteland at least in part of his own making.

In *Love and Anarchy* the prostitute Salome (Melato again) is the only character who knows that a life without commitment is not worth living. She speaks for Wertmuller, insisting that those people who—like Mimi and later Pasqualino—abstain from the struggle will only themselves be destroyed. With Tunin (Giannini), Salome plans the assassination of Mussolini, an act which could have avoided much suffering—although at the end Wertmuller disassociates herself from terrorism and assassination as political methods by quoting a title from Malatesta, who died in 1932: "The assassins were wrong but should be remembered as saints."

Only the woman Salome sustains her resolve, the determination that the butcher Mussolini be destroyed. But Tunin's luxuriant mistress Tripolina stands in her path, preventing her from waking him on the fateful morning. The opportunity to kill Mussolini passes. Tunin will be tortured anyway; better that he at least have achieved the goal which would have prevented so much pain for others. Wertmuller has given it to Salome alone to know that some ideals are worth dying for like a dog. If she knew how to use a pistol, she cries frantically, she would do it herself. Tripolina replies that "there have been wars since time began," an argument she uses to justify her and Tunin's having chosen love before commitment.

Salome, also a member of the antifascist resistance, is the only character clear-headed enough to see the urgency of the task. She will not risk falling in love at this moment and she is far from the wormlike (Wertmuller's term) Mimi and Pasqualino who live only for their own survival. Salome is there in Wertmuller's canon to prove that we can be better, that we need not be reduced to the level of a Pasqualino seducing the Ilse Koch-like Amazon Nazi. Women like Fiore and Salome, rich in consciousness and purpose, know better.

But does her portrayal of the wealthy shrew Raffaella in *Swept Away* (played by Melato) nevertheless stamp Wertmuller a traitor to her sex? Much has been made of Wertmuller's explanation that this woman is "a symbol of bourgeois enlightenment. She represents bourgeois society, therefore she represents the man . . . The Mariangela Melato character was really a man!" In part the disassociation of her sexuality from her intellect has so enraged critics, for Raffaella in the early scenes of the film speaks truths with which Wertmuller clearly concurs. They reveal her to be the most sophisticated commentator in the film on the Italy of her time, particularly on the hypocrisy of the Communist party.

"You call yourselves Communists but you flirt with the Vatican and vote against divorce," she scoffs. She calls Stalin "the genius of artistic disorder." Loud and full of vitality, she asks, "Did Stalin play the Balalaika when he signed death sentences?" That this intelligent woman should degrade her servants and later revel in her own sexual abuse seems incomprehensible, and hence dishonest. And what, anyway, did Wertmuller mean when she called Raffaella a "man"? Was she not simply evading her own misogyny?

It is absurd to see the commandant of Seven Beauties *only as a woman, as if all politics were sexual politics. This individual first and foremost represents the impermeable cruelty of the Nazis. In her person, repulsive as it is, she becomes a visual image of the vision with its readiness to exterminate—a village of Jews, a couple of insignificant Italian deserters and a principled Spanish anarchist.*

What happens when Raffaella is "swept away" is far more complex, for she evokes an entire culture (as does the commandant in *Seven Beauties)*. In this sense she stands not for a sex but for a class. The upper-class woman with her rented yacht is privileged enough to have enjoyed

Once she does fall in love with Mimi, Fiore demands his utter devotion, admitting no compromises. Mimi's equal in all ways and his superior in character, Fiore exerts so humanizing an influence on her callow lover that only when she *responds can he make love to her.*

the benefits of a superior education which, in turn, has allowed her not to be deceived by the lies of the defenders of a Stalin. But representing a world in which starving the poor is taken for granted, she is morally lacking.

Once she and the servant she had taunted find themselves on the desert island, power changes hands. The working-class Gennarino, who is ignorant enough to remain a party member despite Stalin's tyranny, is far more equipped than she to survive. Raffaella experiences a dethronement that as much belongs to her class as it does to her as a woman, a class in which men have enjoyed all the power. "You'll be put in jail for letting me starve," she threatens Gennarino. "If there were such a law all the rich would be in jail," he retorts.

But Raffaella has been freed from having to dispense the cruelties of her former life style. This sudden, fortuitous liberation disorients her and releases her as well; it is why she can suddenly exclaim, "I feel swept by destiny into a strange beautiful dream." Wertmuller humanized this loudmouthed woman who had been a victim of her selfish, privileged life by showing that it had been a *strain* on Raffaella to have treated her servants with such scorn.

Overwhelmed by her release from selfishness, Raffaella responds with excess and in extremes, begging Gennarino to "sodomize" her. But Wertmuller is not portraying woman's innate urge to be mastered; she is chronicling the byways of a personal liberation that are accessible to men as well as women were they not to turn their backs on the suffering of their time, the recurrent great theme of all her films. Raffaella, even when she is forced to do the bidding of another, experiences nothing so much as relief.

That Gennarino at first takes delight in humiliating her should not be surprising, for his behavior—like hers—is determined economically. And so he does for awhile, out of frustration over the years when he— the Southern Italian—was slave, and she—representing the high culture of the North—was master. It is not simply a question of man and woman, a point underlined by Wertmuller at the end of the film when we see Gennarino's Sicilian wife (far from the passive, submissive hausfrau) calling the shots and leading him home. Sexual liberation in *Swept Away* is possible for Raffaella and Gennarino because through a set of absurd circumstances each character temporarily becomes able to reverse a demeaning social role.

Wertmuller is in fact the most profound of feminists because she recognizes that the situation of woman is intimately bound up with the social world she inhabits. Raffaella is the victim of the institutions which have both shaped her and which she preserves at the expense of the many. Like Buñuel in *Belle de Jour,* Wertmuller never demeans her women by glorifying perversion for its own sake. Far from reveling in the stereotype of the rich frigid woman kissing the feet of the virile working-class man, she offers Raffaella a chance to liberate herself from the trap of self-hatred that led her to be so enslaved before she left her yacht. Her release comes too late and not without a price; she can now respond sexually only in circumstances under which she is abused.

Raffaella, like so many heroines of serious fiction and films before her, does not become the positive image of woman at the expense of psychological and social credibility. Nor does Wertmuller didactically

The women in All Screwed Up, *made before* Swept Away, *were either whores or maids lusting after a life style exactly like that of their rich employers and more than willing to sacrifice love for possessions. The men, it was pointed out, were the only people capable of love and devotion.*

impose a message that would convince feminists of her sincerity. Raffaella returns to her wealthy husband and privileged life-style, wormlike in her cowardice but no worse, if better, than Pasqualino or Mimi. Like them she tacitly consents to a world epitomized by the Nazi commandant. But it is not being a woman that makes her weak; it is her comforts which have bound her and damaged her capacity to feel. If Raffaella finally could not love and Gennarino could, it is not because she is only a paltry woman, but because her character has been eaten away by a selfish, careless life in a way that his has not.

In Love and Anarchy, *the prostitute Salome . . . is the only character who knows that a life without commitment is not worth living. She speaks for Wertmuller, insisting that those people who—like Mimi and later Pasqualino—abstain from the struggle will only themselves be destroyed.*

Sexual liberation in Swept Away *is possible for Raffaella and Gennarino because through a set of absurd circumstances each character temporarily becomes able to reverse a demeaning social role.*

In the same way it is absurd to see the commandant of *Seven Beauties* only as a woman, as if all politics were sexual politics. This individual first and foremost represents the impermeable cruelty of the Nazis. In her person, repulsive as it is, she becomes a visual image of the Nazi vision with its readiness to exterminate—a village of Jews, a couple of insignificant Italian deserters, and a principled Spanish anarchist. Wertmuller says that she told Shirley Stoler to imitate the facial expression of the wartime Churchill, to appear as impassive and beyond caring as a fanatic or a Buddha. She is made a woman so that Pasqualino can be shown to be betraying himself on the deepest personal level, epitomized by the sexual. That she does not respond despite his frantic efforts is perfectly fitting as further evidence of how deeply he is denying himself by not waging war against these fascists of the spirit and the body.

But more than a woman, this commandant represents what happens when we sit back and permit ourselves to be swept away by evil. For Wertmuller we in the twentieth century—men and women alike—have abstained from this struggle. Far from being a nihilist who sees everything as pointless and delights in demeaning the human race (but most particularly its woman members), Wertmuller offers a most positive vision. She urges simply that we not acquiesce in suffering.

Far from there being only chaos and no clear point of view in her work, Wertmuller provides a highly consistent passionate appeal which admits the simultaneous liberation of women and men. With Wertmuller, who transcends cliché (whether feminist or any other), we are in the presence of a director who speaks to the point of liberation.

Culture, Kubrick, and *Barry Lyndon*

George H. Lewis

In June 1935 William Thackeray's novel *Vanity Fair,* entitled *Becky Sharp* for the screen, saw its first major review in the *New York Times.* "Science and art, the handmaidens of the cinema, have joined hands to endow the screen with a miraculous new element . . . both incredibly disappointing and incredibly thrilling." In 1976 Thackeray's *Barry Lyndon,* as interpreted by Stanley Kubrick, is evoking similar sounds from the critics.

If there is one constant in the criticism of Kubrick's films, it is that his characters are flat and one-dimensional, that he fails to explore the individual psychological implications of the grand environments his films have become. Such criticism is likewise being heard about *Barry Lyndon.*

Typical reviews laud costuming detail, settings, photographic techniques, the total environment of eighteenth century Europe that Kubrick has created. Yet they invariably conclude with a lament that the plot of this three-hour epic is simplistic, and that character development is nonexistent. Some reviewers have wondered why such a one-dimensional actor as Ryan O'Neal was selected for the lead role.

For a student of the humanities involved in debating how successfully or unsuccessfully an artist has presented an especially important wrinkle in the human conditions, and comparing this treatment with past "classic" treatments, this critique of Kubrick makes sense. For a social scientist, on the other hand, this critique is ridiculous.

Kubrick is an artist who recognizes the importance and explores the implications of the political, technological, and cultural structures of contemporary social systems. He is concerned with the social condition of mankind, not the articulation and development of character flaws in an individual, humanistic tradition. As an artist he is operating at a different level than his critics.

*Kubrick has deliberately chosen the vehicle of commonplace—popular culture—
for this film. The plot is simplistic and the characters are one-dimensional precisely because* Barry Lyndon *is an exploration of the power of popular art and
culture in a social system.*

In his most recent films Kubrick has examined the importance of the
cultural structure of a society and its implications in social, political, and
technological spheres. The impact of cultural stereotypes on the future of
the human race is as important in *Dr. Strangelove* as the assertion that a
fail-safe system is less a technological system than a further cultural
stereotype, developed by the political structure to maintain order and
docility in the social system.

In the years succeeding the film Kubrick's Dr. Strangelove, a merging
of the cultural stereotype of the amoral Nazi scientist with Henry
Kissinger, became a potent mythic symbol given flesh and blood—
"Super-K." Given the tone of Kissinger's foreign policy, "how I learned

to love the bomb'' makes even more chilling non-sense in today's reality than in *Dr. Strangelove.*

The use of cultural artifacts in influencing social conditions is examined fully in *Clockwork Orange,* where Kubrick traces the linkages between those individuals excluded by the "establishment" culture and alienated into violence by it and the cultural forms they choose to promote their identities. What Kubrick does to Beethoven in *Clockwork Orange* is exactly what Hitler did to Wagner in the Third Reich.

Even in *2001: A Space Odyssey* Kubrick is underlining the importance of culture—everyday popular culture and its significance—not so much to characters in the film as to characters in the audience. The space station is that much more real because it has familiar corporate names of today—Hilton, Howard Johnson's—tagged to its technological projections.

Popular, everyday culture is crude, but it does reflect the reality of the social system that produces and consumes it. As such it is not threatening to its consumers and can be used, as Kubrick uses it in *2001,* to individualize and make credible this particular personal future. Why else is the space station so familiar than because it moves to the strains of *The Blue Danube?*

The interface between the cultural and social structures of American society is Kubrick's focal point in *Barry Lyndon,* adapted from Thackeray's nineteenth century novel. Kubrick has deliberately chosen the vehicle of commonplace—popular culture—for this film. The plot is simplistic and the characters are one-dimensional precisely because *Barry Lyndon* is an exploration of the power of popular art and culture in a social system.

The film epic takes a lengthy work of popular literature and transports it to the screen, painting a vast and spectacular backdrop for a simplistic story with one-dimensional characters. To be successful the film, as the popular literary work before it, must reflect and affirm basic values of its potential audience. This formula was successful in *Gone With the Wind* and *The Ten Commandments;* it was unsuccessful in *Ben Hur* and *Antony and Cleopatra.* By choosing the film epic for *Barry Lyndon,* Kubrick speaks as loudly via the form of his creation as via its content.

The romantic illusion, so necessary to the successful film epic, is an important part of *Barry Lyndon.* When the American popular mind reflects on the eighteenth century it affirms the culture of the contemporary upper class as both correct and important. There is an awe of anything cultural. If an object is European, it must be art. At the same time that it accepts unquestioningly the validity of such "art," the American consciousness also rejects the concept of inherent superiority reflected by European class structure. The tension in this cultural-structural interface is the key to *Barry Lyndon.*

Casting Ryan O'Neal as Barry Lyndon was not a mistake, as some critics have labeled it, but rather a shrewd and calculated move on Kubrick's part. O'Neal is an American popular culture symbol. He is the "all American boy," slightly uncomfortable in upper-class social situations but learning how to handle them. He has American innocence and lack of concern for social origins *(Love Story)* and the correct degree of American ingenuity to ascend the social ladder *(Paper Moon).* Kubrick cleverly pushes this American pop hero onto the stage of eighteenth century Europe as it exists in the American consciousness, and carefully frames the whole counterpoint as an American film epic.

Kubrick has been praised for his carefully constructed and photographed sets in *Barry Lyndon.* Most critics have awarded him points on the basis of his considerable technical skill. For example, in order to photograph by actual candlelight Kubrick used a custom-built camera employing the fastest lens ever made—50 mm f 0.7.

What these critics have not seen is the cultural import of what he has done. More than one American, when leaving this film, has remarked that "every scene could have been a painting." By posing the actors for an instant prior to action in many scenes, Kubrick emphasizes this point. The scenes look like European paintings of the 1700s and 1800s. Since such paintings are considered art in the American popular mind, and since art is serious and important, so should *Barry Lyndon* be considered.

The problem comes when the story line and character development are seen as crude and simplistic. This incongruity has left many viewers and critics uneasy. They have not yet seen what many social historians have noticed—the tendency for any cultural object, no matter how poorly done, to be accepted by Americans as serious and valid if it is European and over one hundred years old.

Kubrick is suggesting that the form of a cultural object can and does validate its content, and that this validation has serious consequences for society. Can one cast a story reaffirming the power of a sociopolitical class system over even the ultimately innocent and resourceful American O'Neal, and by casting it as art (or "kitsch," as art historians claim) have the American mass audience accept it as a serious and valid comment on the social condition? Kubrick has succeeded in this effort in *Barry Lyndon.*

In *Barry Lyndon* Kubrick attempts to succeed on two levels. First, by manipulating popular cultural stereotypes his audience holds, he is ask-

If an object is European, it must be art. At the same time that it accepts unquestioningly the validity of such "art," the American consciousness also rejects the concept of inherent superiority reflected by European class structure. The tension in the cultural-structural interface is the key to Barry Lyndon.

ing that audience to examine the power of cultural artifacts in shaping their social world. By introducing contradictions, both between form and content and among the stereotypes, he creates a situation that has made critics and audiences uneasy. Hopefully they will examine why they are uneasy, rather than dismissing it as a grand but flawed film. On this point Kubrick has been optimistic, judging from the reviews thus far penned.

Second, Kubrick makes an important political point in *Barry Lyndon*. The reality showing through the paint and powder of his staged sets and actors is one of class, caste, and power. It is obvious to talk of O'Neal as being transported to eighteenth century Europe, where Kubrick can examine the American character in an alien social structure. But what about turning the situation around?

Kubrick has transported eighteenth century Europe to contemporary America. Suddenly the interface is immediately relevant to our present social situation. Is egalitarianism in America like the powder, paint, and genteel manners of Kubrick's Europe—wisps of cultural imagination buttressed by the insecurity and wishful thinking of the American people? Is the reality, like the chafed cheeks and ugly undertones of *Barry Lyndon* that from time to time tear through the cultural fantasy, one of power and social class in America hiding behind analogously compelling cultural cliches, but potent enough to strike down even a Ryan O'Neal?

The dueling shot that propels O'Neal into the upper social strata at the beginning of *Barry Lyndon* is one of dried sheep-dip. The shot that cuts him down at the close of the film is raw, savage lead. As long as Americans continue to believe in the illusion of romantic love, Kubrick is saying, they will never realize that it is power—in the end—that means never having to say you're sorry.

Black Spookery:
Blacula, Dracula A.D. 1972

Judith Clavir

Horror films are supernatural reflections of social conditions. The specific conditions of people's lives create for moviemakers a battleground for the ultimate struggle of good against evil, of the forces of Life against Living Death. The history of horror flicks is a history of first recognizing the existence of this battle and then projecting fears and fantasies larger and more horrible than life. *Dracula A.D. 1972* and *Blacula* are organic products of this decade's resolution of that historic struggle.

In 1818 Mary Shelly wrote *Frankenstein,* which she subtitled *The Modern Prometheus.* She wrote it in thirty-six hours on a bet from several male poets of the day as to who could write the most terrifying tale. And Bram Stoker wrote *Dracula* in 1897, taking for his model Vlad the Impaler, a fifteenth-century Romanian prince. So by the beginning of the twentieth century, a major arena for the titanic and unceasing struggle against evil was defined by the birth of these creatures.

At first the battle appeared wrapped in the long cloak of racist anti-Semitism. Dracula and other monsters first appeared in German movies in the 1910s and 1920s. The *Nosferatu* (1922) vampire is the traditional caricature of the Jew—hooked nose, lascivious and bloodthirsty. In the first version of *Der Golem* (1915) a Jewish monster is brought to life by a kindly German antiquarian. The Golem falls in love with his creator's daughter and becomes uncontrollable in a fine example of the "sexual prowess" of oppressed minorities. He is eliminated—in a dramatic preview of the Third Reich.

By the 1960s a satiric version of vampire anti-Semitism had appeared. In the Roman Polanski film *Fearless Vampire Killers,* the Jewish vampire, when confronted with a cross held by a trembling victim says with some historical justification, "Lady, have you got the wrong vampire!" The triumph of Christian goodness is the consistent theme of early horror movies. The 1931 Universal Pictures' version of *Dracula* with Bela Lugosi in the title role plays out the conflict with both sides clearly defined—the malevolent bloodsucker is vanquished by Daylight and the Cross of Christ.

The Frankenstein films of the thirties mythologized Mary Shelly's well-meaning doctor seeking to create a perfect being to serve humanity. The message is clear—life can only be created by God, not man. As Boris Karloff's stitched and shaking hand pulls the switch that will blow up the laboratory in the last scene of *Bride of Frankenstein* (1935) he says to the repentant Baron: "No, you go. It is better that we [The Living Dead] really die."

Meanwhile back in the real world of the American thirties the Depression, unemployment, dust bowl refugees and Wall Street suicides became the daily dose of horror. In Germany, while people were gassed for the good of mankind, Hitler tried to create not just the perfect person, but the master race.

Were the moviegoing Americans who paid millions of dollars during this period looking only for a means of escape from the drudgery and calamity of daily existence? Escapist movies are bland bubble-gum masterpieces which, at their best, transport you to the Land of Oz through a field of opium poppies where the greatest danger is a wicked but meltable witch, and where the greatest desire is to return safely home to Kansas. Here too, supernatural forces are overcome. When Dorothy and her friends pull back the curtain and expose the Wizard, dependent on electronic marvels to achieve his mystical majesty, we become aware of our own human strength. Courage, humanity and creativity lie in mortal reach inside ourselves. The battle is to expose and confront the sham of supernatural terrorism, a terrorism which is not so terrifying after all.

Films like *Dracula* and *Frankenstein* provide a broader and deeper reassurance about the direction of the world. Escapist, yes, but horror films were also one of the safe ways Americans could face the reality they were experiencing. Insecurities were assuaged. When Dracula dies by the cross, moviegoers were reassured that, no matter how great the odds, Christian good will triumph. And the defeat of Germany proved once again that no man, no matter how powerful and even in God's name, could go against Divine Will and create a perfect being.

In the 1950s the evil of communism haunted and materially changed conditions in Europe and Asia and crept into the American psyche. Masses of people feared that their country would become dominated by alien ideas and subversives who would take over by mysterious forces of infiltration they could not control. Politically they looked for reas-

The profitability of black filmmaking, together with the search for black identity, has given rise to Blacula, *an American-produced film using Hammer techniques and a black vampire hero.*

surance in McCarthyism, J. Edgar Hoover and Grandfather Eisenhower in the White House. Cinematically, they purged left-wing elements from Hollywood and produced science-fiction movies like *The Thing* (1951) and *Invasion of the Body Snatchers* (1956). The final line in this great film of how alien invaders seize the minds of upstanding white

Americans is "Call the FBI." The subversives don't stand a chance against J. Edgar's clean-cut Christian crusade.

(In the middle fifties a British company, Hammer Films, began reissuing Frankenstein and Dracula movies.) Hammer's genius is taking the original formula and producing high quality, low budget movies. Hammer is now heavily invested with American capital. (In these films, the monster Frankenstein looks more and more like a scarred and ugly human being, an outcast, a freak, and less and less like a hulking creature from hell. Dracula, although eternal and Undead, loses many nonhuman qualities—he can no longer become a bat and fly away, he cannot become a werewolf, and his approach to biting women is strikingly seductive. The Hammer films are shot in the English countryside as opposed to the more surreal, created sets of the Hollywood thirties. The blood is shown in bright red abundance, not hinted at.

Today, after four years of a Republican administration, a prolonged, bloody and seemingly unstoppable war, little change in the real position of blacks in America, the Death of God—all these combining into a growing sense of powerlessness to the people—the titanic battle of the thirties has once again appeared. The forces of Life and goodness battle the Living Dead and evil, updated in Vistavision and Zenith Chromacolor. And Hammer films are becoming extraordinarily popular through double bills and late night television reruns.

The character of who wins out in the struggle between good an evil is changing. Baron Von Frankenstein has today become a more exacting scientist, a more rational gentleman—Christian Barnard-like. He is less a possessed, frenzied intellectual who has gone crazy on his own ideas. But it is Count Dracula who has won the popularity contest of monster superstars. Dracula is powerful, sexual, mysterious, attractive—and he gets things done. No longer the obvious evil villain of the thirties, today's Count gives America's moviegoers a model, a means of supernatural survival in a world almost devoid of goodness.

The profitability of black filmmaking, together with the search for black identity has given rise to *Blacula,* an American-produced film using Hammer techniques and a black vampire hero. An African prince and his bride come to the original Count Dracula's castle to negotiate ending the slave trade. But the Count gets turned on the by the black woman and expresses his deep ideological commitment to slavery. He transforms the Prince into a vampire and, in true slavemaster fashion, chains the black man inside a coffin, forever unable to satisfy his blood lust. Some twenty years later a gay, biracial antique-dealing couple buy up the contents of the castle, transport them to America and loose the black vampire on an unsuspecting Watts.

After a good deal of difficulty, an "integrated good"—in the persons of a black police doctor and a white police inspector—manage to wipe out the plague. But modern racism must be overcome before Christianity can be in any way a viable weapon. "Could this be the work of the Panthers?" asks the white police inspector. The struggle for black identity in the sixties and seventies is a real struggle for power, not for abstract self-definition, but for ways to manipulate and control reality. Blacula is Shaft's supernatural brother, combining good and evil in powerful opposition to the man. His image is more positive than Superfly—he deals in bloody revenge for his enslavement, not cocaine. Forthcoming productions of black monster movies include *Son of Blacula* and *Blackenstein*. What specific role these monsters will play in the black struggle for national liberation is as yet unclear.

In *Dracula A.D. 1972* the indomitable Count rises from his grave (again) summoned by a Mansonesque hippie and his cultish friends. Bored with acid, sex and British decadence, they are archetypes of disillusioned youth who, no longer believing in good, want to identify with evil. They trip out in the unhallowed ground of an abandoned churchyard and revive the Count, who proceeds to drain the blood from the women, turn the men into his mini-vampire servants and confound Scotland Yard. But the scholarly tradition of vampire-fighting in the person of Van Helsing is not dead, and the academic becomes activist and kills the vampire by the tried and true guerrilla method of a stake hidden in the underbrush plunging directly through his heart.

But Van Helsing also has a very hard time of it. Dracula is defeated, but not without a warning. "How dare you oppose me," says the Count, "I who have ruled nations."

The present popularity of these two films indicates that Dracula will rise from his grave again and again and again. The same process of death and rebirth occurred in the thirties. But now each time the Count comes back stronger, and more charismatic, building for himself an ever widening base of popular support. Both Christopher Lee's Dracula and William Marshall's Blacula are tall stunning men with a compelling, sexually polymorphous blood lust. Vanquished easily by Christian good forty years ago, today the Count is able to rip silver crosses off virginal necks with only a slight burn to the hands. As people are becoming increasingly cynical about the possibility of goodness triumphing anywhere in the universe, they are being more and more reassured by an attractive and efficacious evil.

In the 1970s, an era of secular technology, hopelessness, heroin and quaalude, Living Death is for many a not so unattractive solution.

Recent Trends in Pornographic Films

Joseph W. Slade

Mindful of competition in an uncertain economy, producers of pornographic films have begun to use increasingly bizarre acts as drawing cards for audiences satiated with the fairly conventional sex that has dominated commercial porno since it surfaced in theaters about seven years ago. Now that every American housewife knows what "deep throat" refers to, filmmakers, i.e., producers of heterosexual films for a mass market, are casting about for kinkier fantasies.

When speaking of bizarre acts—be they deviant, aberrant, perverted or just plain unusual—we must observe that some once regarded as such have been so thoroughly assimilated into the genre that they are *outré* no longer. Fellation to ejaculation, which takes place in the mouth or over the face of the female, usually called a "splash scene," and double fellation, in which the female sucks on two penises simultaneously, fall into this category. So does group sex in large multiples, although threesomes are preferred because they are more easily photographed and because viewers cannot always identify with exponential combinations. Lesbian couplings have always been a staple of the heterosexual stag film, presumably because, as Philip Wylie once surmised, the male voyeur believes he is getting two fantasy girls for the price of one.

Some acts are properly characterized as gimmicks, rather than perversions. Cases in point are Jaime Gillis's insertion of his entire forearm into Rita Davis's vagina in *Love Bus* (1974), or Jody Maxwell's singing while she fellates a male in *Portrait* (1974), not to mention the enormous penises (if we may call them gimmicks) of Marc Stevens and John Holmes, both of whom have done yeoman service in their choice of profession. One of the changes time and public acceptance have wrought in the realm of pornography is that actors and actresses are no longer anonymous; some, like Marilyn Chambers, have become household

121

names, and three, Linda Lovelace (*Inside Linda Lovelace*), Marc Stevens *(10-1/2)* and Tina Russell *(Porno Star)* have published their memoirs.

The most clever of recent gimmick-oriented films is *The Hottest Show in Town* (1975), produced by Drs. Phyllis and Eberhard Kronhausen, psychology's gifts to the pornographic scene, through a complicated arrangement between a Swiss-Danish company and *Screw* magazine of New York. Like an earlier *Screw* film, *It Happened in Hollywood* (1973), *The Hottest Show in Town* is a spoof of sexuality, albeit in dubious taste. Perhaps the funniest moment occurs when the Kronhausens, looking solemn, introduce the film with the shop-worn excuse that pornography is a therapeutic way of forcing humans to take sex less seriously and with some nonsense about the sociological necessity of exploring the hidden sensuality of that old institution, the circus. The circus is a Danish one, on the verge of bankruptcy. To get it back in the black, the owner replaces the standard three rings with erotic hijinks and sexual feats. Gimmicks being what they are, they actually reduce the frequency of hard-core contact and lead to good-natured horsing around—in one instance quite literally, when a herd of horses watches deadpan as a stallion attempts to mount a mare.

Much of the footage is given over to traditional circus acts performed in the nude: a high-wire ballet, a trapeze act; a girl disrobed by doves, a knife-thrower hurling blades at a naked assistant. In between are squeezed more bizarre skits: clowns insert glowing light bulbs into the vaginas and anuses of girls kneeling in a row, a strong man holds aloft a platform on which a threesome copulates, a juggler races to climax with his partner before balanced plates can fall to the ground, and, in the most touted situation, two dwarfs have intercourse, which should lay to rest the myth that dwarfs are more potent than the rest of us. In spite of these entertaining novelties, *The Hottest Show* is seriously flawed by poor editing, but audiences enjoy its humorous perspective. Doubtless it is especially gratifying to males who as boys sat in the bleachers hoping the bareback lady's tights would split.

Without the expertise of the Kronhausens, who have established a museum of erotica in San Francisco, or the resources of *Screw,* which has a finger on the erotic pulse of the East, most porno producers, while they want to flavor their films with the bizarre, are aware that many aberrations are specialized tastes and do not wish to gamble on turning off a majority of potential audiences by catering to too narrow a minority. Fortunately for them, a testing-ground is available requiring very simple market research techniques to exploit. To learn where the 16 or 35mm theater-grade, full-length heterosexual stag film is heading, one has only to visit the 8mm film arcades dotting Times Square, where streams of men drop quarters into private booth projectors to view the lucrative short films fed into the machines in "loops." While most of them are domestic, at the moment foreign loops go over well; the latter do not come from Denmark, which apparently has tired of porno, but from an emergent pornographic axis stretching loosely from Germany to Holland to Sweden. The loops vary in quality, but what makes them interesting is the diversity of their subjects; it is in this respect that they function as bellwethers for the theater-length film. In short, whatever deviations prove popular in the arcades will show up within six months in New York movie houses.

Strolling through an arcade's rows of projectors, one has merely to notice which are most heavily patronized. A large arcade offers something for everybody, from the hetero- to the homosexual, the former being our concern. One or two booths will exhibit films for pedophiles, although arcade owners tend to be cautious here. Given the murkiness of obscenity statutes, one of the few certain ways to get convicted on a New York indictment is to purvey pornography involving children—but only if the kids are white and American.

Beyond that caveat, almost anything goes: men, singly or in groups, copulating with menstruating women, fat women, tattooed women or pregnant women. Interracial sex is popular, the most prevalent mix being black and white, with Orientals coming up fast. Bestiality is common, but so far extensive intercourse with animals has formed the basis for only one full-length film in New York, a Danish import starring a girl named Bodil Joensen, who takes on a dog, a donkey and a pig. *Animal Lover* played to a packed—if small—house at the Mini-Cinema for twelve months in 1973-74.

Among the most persistent of bizarre practices in loops are "golden showers," a euphemism for men and women urinating on each other. As a consequence, urophilia and urolagnia have found their way into the full-length film, most often as supplements to conventional intercourse. On the other hand, coprophagia, or a delight in excrement, has made no headway in either 8 or 35mm, nor, after a brief vogue, have enemas.

Weird as these matters sound, there is about the loops a curious air of innocent experimentation, as if their producers were simply trying to assess the predilections of a heterogeneous audience. In terms of sheer bulk, these sexual artifacts of the American 1970s might be compared to that other great flowering of the esoteric blue 8mm film, the Cuban period of the 1920s and 1930s, but the American strain, for all its seediness, lacks the decadent ambience of the other. Only serendipity can account for some loops. This reviewer's favorite is a recent arrival in which a nude man and woman do nothing but lick each other's nostrils

Mindful of competition in an uncertain economy, producers of pornographic films have begun to use increasingly bizarre acts as drawing cards for audiences satiated with fairly conventional sex that has dominated commerical porno since it surfaced in theaters about seven years ago.

until one sneezes; it recalls the dated theories of Wilhelm Fliess, Freud's friend, the proponent of nasal eroticism and originator of Fliess's Syndrome.

Fetishes, such as transvestitism and other garment fixations, are negligible components of the loops (if only because those subject to them rarely wish to see genital sex) except as kinky embellishments of other practices. Leather and rubber, for example, usually appear conjoined with sado-masochism (S-M). Here we enter an area at once significant and confusing—but illustrative of trends in modern movies. Sado-masochists of all stripes share a desire to debase and thereby exalt. The paradox is traditional, reflective of fundamental tenets of a Christian culture: suffering both reminds us of the authentic limitations of the self and allows us to transcend those limitations. Through degradation comes triumph.

Assuming that culture defines eroticism and that eroticism centers on the conflict of the self with itself and with other selves in an arena in which dominance and submission are constants, the S-M crowd may come closer to an apprehension of raw eroticism than the "normal" majority. According to Georges Bataille, the foremost authority on eroticism of our time, "Eroticism, unlike simple sexuality, is a psychological quest independent of the natural goal: reproduction and the desire for children." If that be correct, then the sado-masochist benefits from the advantage of having sidestepped the reproductive side of human sexuality; he is concerned almost wholly with a pure form of sexual tension. He is obsessed with limits, with how far he can transgress the taboos his society has fashioned.

Bataille speaks at length of the erotic necessity of approaching taboos in order to transgress them, to find out what the limitations of the self are. Real eroticism, he says in *Death and Sensuality,* always calls for "an infraction of the laws of taboo." Another way of putting it is that true eroticism always hinges on guilt. It can and should be argued that any significant sexual encounter turns on the perception of limitations. The limitations are those which bound our being and circumscribe our isolation from one another, and a sexual act is an attempt to break down those boundaries, to free ourselves from our isolation and to establish intimate affinity with another.

To shatter the parameters of being and to try to violate the boundaries of other selves traditionally have been regarded by Westerners as dangerous and irrational. So disruptive is sexual impulse, so close does it approach disorder that in our culture, orgasm, *le petit morte,* is often equated with death and annihilation of the self. In reaching climax, we lose ourselves in an ecstasy that acknowledges and deliberately oversteps the boundaries of the self as it approaches nothingness until at last we draw back in horror and guilt at our own flight toward extinction—and in retreat find a new awareness of our separate identities.

Unlike the sado-masochist, most of us do not demand, although we usually enjoy, dominance and submission; nor do we respond to the same metaphors for the sexual act, let alone the paraphernalia, the whips and chains, that he requires. The ritualistic nature of S-M fantasies creates for the S-M freak a community of pain; he appears to join others in mutual complicity to liberate the self. To the "normal" viewer, the S-M rituals, say a stylized fantasy of a schoolmaster punishing a child, seem quaint, almost harmless, especially when measured against the explicit and much more "real" violence of the legitimate film and television show. Indeed, the tolerant viewer may be turned off if the ritual does not sufficiently disguise brute force.

With a few ugly exceptions, arcade loop violence is tame—as yet. While one might occasionally see a woman's breasts burned with cigarettes, flagallation is typically and obviously faked with lipstick welts. Broadly speaking, there is even less "real" violence in the chic theater film on the order of the highly ritualized *Behind the Green Door* (1972). In the full-length film so far, rape, for instance, has been prized less for its own sake than as an excuse for the dominance the rape occasions and the sex that follows, if such a leaky distinction can hold any water at all. When brutal rapes or beatings do occur, audiences in theaters can take offense.

Such was this reviewer's impression watching *Defiance* (1974), a film produced by Jason Russell (ex-husband of Tina), the plot of which leans heavily on sado-masochism a la de Sade (the full title is *The Defiance of Good)*. In the film, parents mistakenly commit their nubile blond daughter to a New York mental institution, where she is repeatedly and bloodily raped by inmates. A psychiatrist pretends sympathy, removes her from the institution and transfers her to his private sanitarium. There she finds that she has stepped from frying pan to fire when the good doctor breaks her spirit with "discipline," establishes psychological dominance and turns her into a sex-craving object of near-permanent submission.

Sooner or later each member of the doctor's zany household plumbs her charms individually or in a large pile with the girl (Jean Jennings) at the bottom. Once the ritualistic elements come into play, nothing very cruel happens: a slap here or an armtwisting there bring her into line. As a final test, she is supposed to betray her best friend as evidence of her having succumbed utterly to amorality (she does not—redeeming social importance).

Russell tries to present a rationale for the doctor's behavior. A failed minister, the psychiatrist has brought to sex a messianic streak blunted a bit by his penchant for pompous speeches on the nature of morality. The best sex is cerebral, rather than physical, he says; transcendence lies in degradation and in spurning false labels like good and evil. The audience absorbs the harangues in placidity betokening incomprehension and enjoys the dominance without buying the violence or even its justification.

Defiance notwithstanding, bloody epics are probably not in the offing.

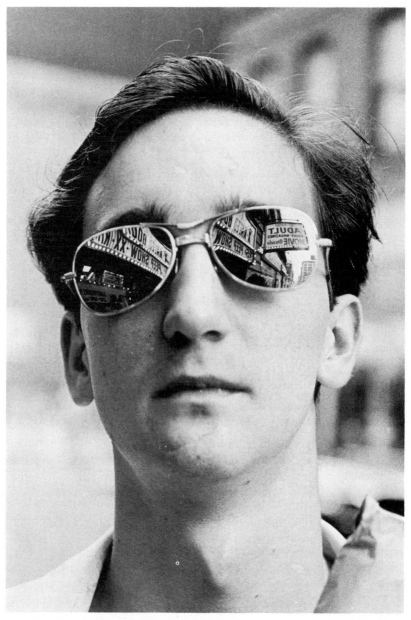

Most porno producers, while they want to flavor their films with the bizarre, are aware that many aberrations are specialized tastes and do not wish to gamble on turning off a majority of potential audiences by catering to too narrow a minority.

Despite its erosion in society at large and in the "legitimate" film, the taboo against graphic abuse of females is holding, probably because of the special expectations and the romantic quasi-reverence toward sex which socially conditioned "regular" viewers bring to the porno houses with them. This taboo is not holding so firmly as the one against excrement, but it is holding nonetheless, and sophisticated producers are aware of the resistance to genuine brutality in the genre. What those filmmakers are looking for is a deviation which subtly transgresses a fairly universal taboo, one that the average audience can find exciting without being completely repulsed.

The taboo to be deviated from must be traditional to our culture, for only thus can it stimulate large numbers of people, although obviously there is no hope that it can turn on all. It must draw the participant, or in this case the viewer, who can participate vicariously, into that complex relationship between acceptable guilt and desire in order to foster the sense of mystery, the sense of complicity which informs eroticism.

If the mystery is to resonate, another essential attribute will have to be a slightly sinister quality, so that an association with death or extinction will not be strained. Moreover, as Bataille has pointed out, to be effective it must be a taboo whose transgression can be rationalized or even denied. For example, nudity is taboo in our culture even though the taboo has been considerably weakened, but it has long been possible to justify it by referring to nudity as natural, aesthetic and even divine. It is virtually impossible to convincingly rationalize beating someone to a pulp, however, and scarcely less easy to justify a fascination with excrement.

For most males, these two taboos—against violence toward women and against excrement—are matched in force only by the prohibition against homosexuality. It would be nice, then, if the all-purpose taboo could encompass aspects of all three. In addition, considering the nature of eroticism as Bataille outlines it, the taboo could only gain if the deviation were divorced from reproduction.

Just how one calibrates degrees of deviation from the norm naturally depends on personal as well as societal mores, but a growing tolerance on the part of individual and mass has rendered acceptable what once were shameful acts. Pornographers know this better than anyone else, although it would be absurd to insist that they think along these precise lines; after all, the search for an all-purpose taboo is not the search for the double helix. The fast buck is still the principal motive behind the pornographer's quest for variety, with opportunism a close second. Intent on serving up a sexual salad, the amateur may hit upon it just as quickly as the pro. At the same time, neither economics nor accident explain the direction the contemporary porno film is taking. However one wishes to regard the matter, a search has been going on and it seems to have been successful.

Last year, when *Screw* conducted an informal poll on what (primarily male heterosexual) audiences would like to see on their local porno screens, violence and rape were at the bottom of the list. At the top were conventional intercourse, fellatio—and anal intercourse. That a preference for the latter act is swelling rapidly has been evident in the arcades for the last eighteen months. The largest number of quarters go into machines showing "fanny films," in which males copulate anally with females.

Anal intercourse is probably the number one "unnatural act" in Western civilization; so strong is the taboo that its legal definition is masked in terms like sodomy, a label broad enough to include bestiality, oral sex and homosexuality in most states. Were one to cast about for a simpler name, one should have to use pedication, which is too stilted, or buggery, which is too English, apparently, to find acceptance among Americans; one might as well stick to anal intercourse. For all its strength, the taboo can be rationalized or seems to have been a sizable segment of the population. Any number of modern sex primers urge us to tinker with each other's backsides or at least to look benignly on those who do, and Salvador Dali has hailed a preference for anal intercourse as a wave of the future, but statistics on its present-day practice are inconclusive.

A discussion of anality is complicated by conflicting theories concerning its implications. At one pole are the Freudians, who believe that anality derives from psychic inducements, that an interest in the anus suggested an arrested infantility and that any such fascination can be associated in our culture with the death instinct and all sorts of unpleasant things. A host of theories has flourished since Freud took on the subject in the first decade of this century. Most of them occupy the ground between Freud and the other extreme adopted by the Kinseyians, who take their cue from the 1948 and 1953 studies, in both of which Kinsey maintained that because the anus was obviously full of nerve endings, it was an erogenous area like others subject to tactile stimulation, and required no special theory to explain its eroticism. Similarly, a customary contemporary rationalization is that anal intercourse is a method of birth control; it permits pleasure without danger of reproduction, a factor which doubtless enhances its eroticism.

At any rate, anal intercourse is the leading deviation spicing contemporary porno films. As far as porno performers are concerned, it is simply a special skill that can be mastered. Most of the major starlets are "three-way" girls, i.e., they engage in oral, vaginal or anal intercourse on demand. Linda Lovelace, whose session of anal intercourse in *Deep Throat* so revolted New York Trial Judge Tyler, has rated oral, anal and vaginal sex in that order of personal preference. Other popular actresses who have not drawn the line at anal intercourse are Jacquie Brody *(Sodom and Gomorrah)*, Jody Maxwell *(Portrait)*, Susan York *(Fulfillment)*, Sandy Foxx *(Teenage Nurses)* and Georgina Spelvin *(The Devil in Miss Jones)*. The dean of American porno directors, Gerard Damiano *(Deep Throat, The Devil in Miss Jones, Memories Within Miss Aggie, Portrait)*, includes explicit scenes of anal intercourse in all of his movies.

So does Lasse Braun, Damiano's counterpart in Europe. An Italian named Alberto Ferro, he adopted the pseudonym to take advantage of the cachet the public attributes to Scandinavians. Braun, tri-based in Amsterdam, Cologne and Stockholm, is staggeringly prolific of technically expert films. Nearly all of them, most of which have entered the United States in 8mm, employ heavy anal intercourse.

So aware is Braun of the trend that he has shot an 8mm series called *Deep Arse*. Only two of his full-length productions, *The Second Coming of Eve* (1974) and *French Blue* (1974—also known as *Penetration*), have turned up in theaters here, but the latter's anality more than makes up for any others. *French Blue*'s star is Brigette Maier, a former American prostitute turned *Penthouse* cover girl (July, 1974) and doyenne of European porno actresses; she is also the world's undisputed queen of anal intercourse. Because of her liberal sexual views, *Screw* has described her as an "anal anarchist," which must be some sort of end to politics (pun intended).

French Blue develops along the documentary lines classic to porno films; a second camera follows Braun as he makes a movie. In between "takes" are inserted as padding scenes from some of Braun's other films. The focus of the "exterior" film is the shooting of one of the *Deep Arse* series, a special one. In contrast to the more common practice of having one male copulate vaginally with a female while another enters her anus, in this session two men attempt to anally penetrate Maier *simultaneously*. Braun and the two males joke about the implied homosexuality of their activity. Although both men anally copulate with her singly, they do not manage the contortions necessary to do so together. Maier considers it all great fun, but is disappointed at the failure to achieve what she thinks would have been a "historical first." From her standpoint, the Kinseyians are correct; she likes anal intercourse because it feels good—she rationalizes the taboo. While the endless talk of technique and the documentary approach prevent any significant treatment of eroticism, *French Blue,* immensely popular, will probably become a top-grosser.

Not all starlets are as casual about the act as Maier. Other directors use anal intercourse sporadically because of the difficult camera angles and the resistance of some performers. Vagina and anus are so close together that the camera angles must be carefully chosen so that the viewer can see what is going on. The act is probably uncomfortable in the best of circumstances, which is why some actresses refuse outright, insist on a relaxed mood—not easy to achieve in the chaos of filming—or limit themselves to analingus, digital caresses or penetration with a vibrator, the latter appliance being as much a standby of the porno film as it is of the modern American home. But the pain—real or feigned—on the faces of the women is also one reason why anal intercourse appears so often.

In this respect and in others, far from settling any dispute between the Freudians and the Kinseyians, the new emphasis on anality raises questions. Heterosexual audiences by and large seem to be turned off by extreme violence, by overt male homosexuality and by blatant scatology, but are stimulated by an activity which is associated with all three. The associations crop up repeatedly in the anality of modern films. The last example is *Masters of Discipline* (1974), produced for Athena Films (to suggest "Greek" sex) of San Francisco by two women, Katrina Lee and Mary Thomas. Execrably photographed, with an even worse soundtrack, *Masters of Discipline* contains three segments, in each of which the same two psychotic brothers capture and torment a female, giving as their reason some sin on the part of the woman. In the most interesting sequence, the victim is the brothers' sister. The titillation of incest is augmented by religious fanaticism; she is "chastised" for being absent from home when their aged parents died in a fire by being forced to wash her brothers' feet with her hair and being tied to a cross while the two "mortify" her flesh.

In the main, the "torture" is unconvincing. The males clamp clothespins on the sister's breasts, pull her hair and tie her up with elaborate boy scout knots. Obviously suffering from a singularly unimaginative form of dementia, the brothers rack their brains (along with their sister) for something really terrible to do to her. Predictably, the worst they can think of is anal intercourse. They reach the same conclusion in the other two segments, involving women they "punish" for their "loose" sexual habits. As they probe the women's rectums with first a broomstick, then a carrot and finally their penises, they appear to corroborate the Freudians, for they resemble children playing doctor.

The action is characterized by two not very subtle nuances: ritual and homosexuality. The ritualistic aspect has the effect of reducing the violence of what would otherwise simply be rape, particularly since none of the women resist; indeed, they appear to concur in the "justice" of their punishment in the best masochistic manner. "Now I'm going to twist her nipples, Jason," says one brother, and the victim obligingly squeals on cue as her part of the charade, but makes no further protest. The anal intercourse is simply part of the scenario that allows the violence to shade into psychological dominance. The homosexuality is apparent in the sexual congress known as a "sandwich," in which one brother enters the female vaginally, the other anally (neither being as ambitious as Braun or Maier). Over the shoulder of the middle of the sandwich, the brothers prattle at each other about redemption, suffering and guilt—in deliberately falsettoed voices. The girl serves to a degree as an excuse for the eroticism between the males.

What emerges from a consideration of this film and others too numerous to mention is that anal intercourse between males and females often sublimates male homosexuality and hostility toward females. It gratifies predominantly male audiences interested in both homosexuality —which they regard in overt form as threatening or disgusting—and domination of females—any violent form of which they consider morally or socially unacceptable. As for the third aspect of anality—its scatological associations—we can only observe that most "fanny films" are antiseptic. Only rarely is a penis withdrawn from an anus soiled, and then almost always to vocal or visible disapproval from the audience, as if the viewers had caught a glimpse of that "horror" Bataille says hovers around deliberate transgressions of taboo. Almost surely the notion that anal intercourse is "dirty" contributes to its appeal. Our culture has always acknowledged, nay, insisted on the connection between sexuality and filth.

It is tempting to think of the Supreme Court as having connived at the association of sex and dirtiness by accepting at one stage of its endless attempt to define obscenity the phrase "a shameful or morbid interest in nudity, sex or excretion," but a better whipping boy is St. Augustine, who liked to remind humans that "we are born between feces and urine," and who helped to disseminate some rather strange ideas through the centuries that followed.

In a larger sense it is silly to assign blame at all, since according to Norman O. Brown—who does get in some licks against Luther in *Life Against Death*—the Protestant impulse which led to our civilization, with all its faults and virtues, owes much of its energy to the taboo against anality. Both genitality and anality have been traditionally associated with man's animalistic side and with irrationality, dirtiness and death. Both genitality and anality, but especially the latter, have been repressed in the service of rational, orderly Protestant systemization. Brown's is a Freudian interpretation of history, which also acknowledges the parallels between the Freudian scheme of genitality and anality and Weberian theories of social and political rationalization.

Considered in that light, calling Brigette Maier an "anal anarchist" is not so absurd as first it seems, since anality, because it has been repressed, is dangerous for that reason. If the relationship between Protestantism and repressed anality is so close, then anality loosed from repression can be powerful to the point of political statement, one supposes, and, considering what passes for political statement these days, Maier's is as good as many others.

Perhaps anality does represent a crack in the system. Brown has detailed the religious anathemas heaped upon anality; for Protestants, a fascination with the anus is not only a danger to civilizing impulses, but also a sin against God. Thus, because the anus became Satan's province, says Brown, "The Devil is a middle term connecting Protestantism and anality." So construed, the taboo against anality is basic to our culture; it has psychological, sociological, political, metaphysical and religious meanings, and that is covering a lot of bases.

Rather than getting lost in historical analysis, however, we can content ourselves with some random observations:

- In the classic written pornography of our culture, anal intercourse plays a major role in the works of de Sade, in Pierre Louys's *Trois Filles* and in Pauline Reage's *Story of O,* to name only three of our most celebrated erotic authors (perhaps the fact that they are all French helps to explain why Lasse Braun could call his move *French* rather than *Greek Blue*; the Greeks never felt guilty about anal intercourse). As each uses it, anal intercourse enhances the resonance of degradation and dominance, homosexuality and/or scatology, and is frequently closely connected with a death instinct inherent in the characters.

- Without exception, the examples of anal intercourse on the porno film markets today originate in countries with strong Protestant traditions: America, Germany, the Netherlands, Sweden, Denmark.

- The most popular soft-core pornographic film of this decade, *Last Tango in Paris,* uses anal intercourse as a deviation against taboo. When Marlon Brando simulates the act with Maria Schneider, the idea is that he is trying to reach her, to employ pain to break through their isolation from each other. He later asks her to put her fingers in his anus, again to try to accomplish through pain and debasement a transcendence of limitations. It is a desperate act, dangerous psychologically, as any attempt to break through limitations is; the death of the Brando character is prefigured in that moment.

- The two leading contemporary American novelists, Thomas Pynchon and Norman Mailer, have both progressed toward an examination of anality and anal intercourse in their work. Pynchon employs it in a Weberian context in

Gravity's Rainbow. Mailer concentrates on it twice, the first time in a short story, "The Time of Her Time" (variant title: "The Taming of Denise Gondelman"), in which he explores the homosexual associations of anal intercourse, and the second in *An American Dream,* in which the Jewish-Protestant Rojack copulates with Ruta, the German maid, in her anus, a place he calls the Devil.

While these observations may be overly erudite in a discussion of a limited genre, they should indicate the topicality of the all-purpose taboo and the kind of sparks it can give off; they also tell us something about what is happening in the porno film.

The hard-core movie seems to be turning back in upon itself. When porno first began to be shown in theaters, the apology took a standard liberal form: sex is beautiful, sex is healthy, sex is less obscene than violence, there is nothing dirty about it and so on. Pornographers— and some of the rest of us—are beginning to sense that idyllic sex is simplistic and, from the standpoint of eroticism, simpleminded.

Sex is a medium of communication subject to more distortions than are recognized in modern information or communication theory. Whatever sweet and lovely areas sex may embrace, raised to the plane of eroticism it also encompasses the ripping and tearing of selves; it includes transgression, dominance, submission, hurt. It is a state of permanent ambivalence vibrating between ever-shifting poles. We probably need "perverted" sexual metaphors and raw sexual fantasies as clues to these energies, some of which are decidedly unpretty. Putting aside repugnance at least acquaints us with some of the forces; without the metaphors and the fantasies, we cannot even see.

The feminist will object that these metaphors, specifically ones employing our all-purpose taboo, succeed primarily at the expense of women. She will react against the dominance of women implied in the recent movie trends. Apart from observing flippantly that anal intercourse has the advantage of avoiding the vaginal versus clitoral orgasm dispute entirely and more seriously that eroticism almost always calls for dominance or submission on somebody's part, this writer has no wish to step off a sexist precipice. It is obvious that the all-purpose taboo as described functions chiefly for males; whether it does anything for females is another question. Lois Gould has said ("Pornography for Women," *New York Times Magazine,* March 2, 1975) that women respond powerfully to *Story of O,* and since that novel makes no sense without the anal intercourse that occasions O's degradation and triumph, it might be that women respond to the taboo as well.

There is also some evidence that movie anality is passing into a more complex stage of bisexuality, with females inserting dildos and whatnot into the anuses of their male partners. Maybe we are headed toward a sort of indiscriminate pansexuality in which the genitals are by-passed in favor of a common anality (that might comfort the really militant feminist). In any case, we do not have to endorse anal intercourse or, for that matter, any other deviation from respected taboos.

Does the discovery—or more precisely, since it has had currency in classic pornography—the rediscovery of the all-purpose taboo mean that hard-core porno films can now move foward toward the status of art? In spite of the apparent availability of money and talent, this is doubtful. The immediacy of any explicit hard-core act tends to arrest any possibility of coherent union between the elements of a film. Were we actually to see Brando's penis sliding in the butter in *Last Tango,* the shock of the actual would shatter the film's continuity. Genitals and anuses are as inscrutable as the wooden-faced performers who own them usually are in the porno films made thus far; whatever resonance they convey derives from the shock of exposure and the thrill of transgression, not from the personalities involved. The hard-core film will probably remain a fertile substratum for "legitimate" films. The making of *Last Tango* would have been inconceivable had not pornos prepared the way.

On the other hand, as examples of eroticism distinct from works of art, the hard-core types may be coming of age. In choosing to incorporate ithyphallic material once ragarded as beyond the pale, pornographers are not trying to defile sex so much as to restore a sense of transgression, to sharpen guilt, the psychic censor far more authoritarian than any the Supreme Court would approve. To darken an arena into which too much light has already been shed may be the only way to reestablish mystery and dread. Taboos hold out the promise of resonance and tension, of eroticism itself. Like others that have preceded them, these taboos, including the all-purpose one, may recede with acceptance, but for the time being they are viable and fresh. Having been premised for so long on the assumption that sex was on the side of the angels, the porno films are now receptive to devils.

Disaster Epics:
Cashing in on Vicarious Experience

Roger Shatzkin

Disaster epics have been box-office dynamite since the story of Noah and the Ark. In the movies the genre appears in embryo as early as the Lumière Brothers' *Démolition d'un Mur* (1896) and in more fully developed form in the Babylon sections of Griffith's *Intolerance* (1916). By the Great Depression, the genre had emerged full-blown into talking, singing and dancing extravaganzas, such as *San Francisco* (1936), *The Hurricane,* (1937) and *In Old Chicago* (1938). The pleasure derived from watching things burned, flooded, exploded and smashed from the safety of a theater seat has had long-lived appeal. In the history of films, perhaps only the chase sequence provides as intense a vicarious experience. Thus any notions that the current spate of "disaster" movies represents some new film phenomenon can be dismissed as public relations.

What cannot be dismissed as easily is the continuing ability of the movie industry, as demonstrated by these films, to reach simultaneously for our pulses and our pocketbooks. To borrow from Calvin Coolidge, "The business of Hollywood is business," and on the simplest level, these current incarnations of disaster have proved wildly successful in luring customers to theaters in the midst of an economic depression. Parallels from the Great Depression, such as Warner Brothers' big-production musicals and M-G-M's star-studded spectaculars, prove that Hollywood has had a long history of capitalizing on economic hard times by offering the pertinent escapist relief. Judging from *Variety's* "50 Top-Grossing Films" for the week of April 23, conglomerated Hollywood has shown itself equally capable of squeezing rewards from our "stagflated" economy. *The Towering Inferno* is the largest total grosser on the list, with *Earthquake* in third position, following *Godfather Part II*. Their total gross has reached over $30 million so far. But the reasons for the immense popularity of these films goes beyond regarding them in terms of pure escapism. For escapism, as the American experience in the 1930s demonstrated, subtly but firmly legitimizes the status quo. Paradoxically, disaster films quell anxiety and reinforce an audience's feeling of well-being.

One of the most apparent ways that these films function to assure us that "everything will be all right," is to shift potentially real questions and problems into conventional forms to which we have stock responses. Robert Warshow maintained that the effect of culture in the 1930s was to set this pattern "to distort and eventually destroy the emotional and moral content of experience, putting in its place a system of conventionalized 'responses' . . . [that] relieve one of the necessity of experiencing one's life directly."

It is therefore not surprising that these films are structured in melodramatic "hero-to-the-rescue" forms that go back to D. W. Griffith. They all conform to Griffith's basic principle of the "switchback" between two or more parallel actions, building suspense as each action moves to its culmination. This can be seen most vividly in the crosscutting in disaster films between the growing holocaust and domestic intrigue or between, typically, a man, husband or lover and the woman, wife and/or children he is trying to save. What could be more melodramatic than heroes to the rescue of women and children in peril? *Airport 1975* answers that through one of its characters, a young girl who is a kidney transplant patient. The particular jeopardy here is the added suspense derived from wondering what will get her first—kidney failure or the plane crash. *The Towering Inferno* and *Earthquake* indulge in the even worse and cloying melodramatic sin: pets in peril.

Despite the realism of the illusion and the quite real response of tension that is built up, our innermost understanding of these conventionalized forms blocks empathtic concern. We get stimulated, but held at a distance and insulated from any deeply felt emotions. At the same time, this insulating function is abetted by overkill. The quantities of graphic and excessive physical destruction in these films desensitize us to their impact. As Susan Sontag has noted about science fiction films, "Fantasy can normalize what is psychologically unbearable thereby inuring us to it." Even our implicit understanding of the Hollywood "magic" of special effects undercuts the *trompe l'oeil* illusion and increases our detachment: it is simply fun to watch what we intuitively know (and keep reassuring ourselves) are scale models and trick photography combined to give a horrendously good show.

One's superficial involvement, mitigated and balanced by all these distancing devices, adds up to a wonderful vicarious experience. Viewers can leave the theater feeling numbed and purged, with the notion that they, like their heroes, have survived a holocaust, and that, at least for the moment, their own mundane problems are inconsequential.

Perhaps it is easier to see how we can leave these celluloid apocalypses purged of certain feelings and anxieties than to understand how and why we carry home a sense of renewed optimism. Though not without confusion at times, disaster films offer an ideology based on the models they supply for behavior in the face of emergencies and crises.

By and large, these films propose "good leadership" as the means of getting people out of critical situations. This is somewhat problematic, because in a film such as *The Towering Inferno,* it is clear that civic leader/construction magnate William Holden's greed and subsequent corner-cutting in building the tower have helped to cause the problem in the first place. But this is glossed over; good leaders *can* get us through. Paul Newman is such a dynamic figure as his firm's chief architect in *Inferno,* that when he returns to his office he is literally mobbed by underlings who seem to have been incapable of functioning in his absence. When it comes to extricating people from the burning building, the same emphasis on leadership and expertise prevails. Newman and fire chief Steve McQueen seem to direct the operation single-handedly, with some egalitarian assistance from O. J. Simpson as a heroic security officer, and even a hand from corrupt tycoon Holden, who shows that his courage runs deeper than his passion for a fast buck.

While there is nothing new in Hollywood's proposing good leadership as the solution for complex problems, these films exemplify a new relationship between leaders and the people to be led. Leaders in these films (it should be noted that they uphold the status quo since they are all men) do not appear to be connected to the masses they guide or rescue. Even when these films purport to give us working-class heroes, such as McQueen's tough and decisive fire chief, cutting through all the ruling-class red tape, or George Kennedy's wrongfully maligned law and order cop (in *Earthquake*), it is clear that these figures are already vested with legal authority that sets them apart from the masses. The other leaders in these films such as Newman, and especially Charlton Heston *(Airport 1975, Earthquake),* are vested a priori with charismatic authority. (Occasionally, a character such as Richard Harris's Fallon, the naval bomb expert in *Juggernaut,* combines both types of authority.) Everyone has the added charismatic "otherness" of star quality.

There is no sense then, that a leader emerges from a group of people and can be made in any way by the situation, let alone even crystallize a group's solidarity. Crises arise and certain men of implicit authority are mysteriously there to take control. If one does not listen to them, one

The pleasure derived from watching things burned, flooded, exploded, and smashed from the safety of a theater has had a long-lived appeal. In the history of films, perhaps only the chase sequence provides as intense a vicarious experience.

runs the risk of the poor souls in *The Towering Inferno*, who, unmindful of Newman's and McQueen's order to tie themselves down before the extinguishing flood of water, get washed out of the skyscraper's penthouse like twigs in the path of a tidal wave.

Contrast this to some films from the depression of the 1930s to the prewar 1940s, where at least the impression of democratic process was maintained: Frank Capra's comedies in which ordinary folks such as Mr. Deeds and Mr. Smith could ostensibly lead "the little people" from whom they had emerged, or Ford's *Young Mr. Lincoln* and Hawks's *Sergeant York,* which reenact the mythological emergence of the leader from the common folk. These films from the depression also made reinforcing statements about the nature of leadership and its ability to pull people through hard times. But gauge the distance we have come when, in disaster movies, not even a pretense of representational leadership is asserted. The attempt to portray the "natural" authority of leadership has moved more openly toward authoritarianism.

This inadvertently touches on a deeper and darker pessimism, for the heroes of the latest disaster movies seem stripped even of the traditional justification of a broader "morality" generally conferred upon the authoritarian hero. In W. S. Van Dyke's *San Francisco* (1936), Clark Gable's swaggering saloonkeeper Blackie Norton, is regenerated by his heroic exploits amid the disastrous quake. We know that he has revealed himself worthy of the heroine (Jeanette MacDonald) who had risen out of his class. He is the true American aristocrat, the man of action— whose deeper moral value transcends his outward appearance. Quite to the contrary, Charlton Heston in *Earthquake,* reveals absolutely nothing except a perpetually pained expression for all his heroism. He is hero and authority, but since he has cheated on his meddlesome wife, he is hero as fallen man. At the end of the film, when Heston opts to rescue his wife from a flooded sewer, rather than stay with his new lover, he literally goes right down the drain. Rather than accepting this denouement as the deserts of a Victorian morality (strange in a contemporary film), it should be seen as a cynical indication that the mere fact of leadership no longer implies, either overtly or covertly, a correct moral stance. Good leaders, even heroes, no longer necessarily have *right* on their side; their authority exists divorced from all ethical and democratic contexts.

Occasionally, "good" leaders cannot do it all by themselves. Instead of calling on people to help save themselves, they call on "good" established bureaucracies and governmental agencies. To the rescue come the United States Air Force *(Airport 1975),* the United States Navy and the San Francisco Fire Department *(The Towering Inferno),* the Los Angeles Police Department and the National Guard *(Earthquake)* and the Royal Navy *(Juggernaut).* It seems unimaginable in the world of these films that the people themselves could take charge of their lives, even in the midst of a crisis. In our powerlessness, all we can hope to do is rely upon a good and charismatic leader, aided by the appropriate government agency.

One of the other reinforcing effects of these movies pertains to the types of disaster in which they revel. In terms of human life, they are not convincingly apocalyptic. *Airport 1975* and *Juggernaut* have less than half a dozen fatalities each. In *Earthquake,* the most wildly destructive of these films, one never has a clear idea of the extent of these casualties; instead, one is shown a large group of people receiving medical attention. Fire chief Steve McQueen proudly announces in the closing minutes of *The Towering Inferno* that the "body count" was kept under 200. Except for a few brief scenes in *Earthquake,* there is almost no human suffering or even blood shown explicitly. Like Greek tragedy, the camera turns away from showing actual moments of pain and death at close range.

These films avoid human costs and focus instead upon the destruction of property. The disintegrating, exploding and conflagrating of buildings, lavish apartments, cars, airplanes and helicopters, occupy center stage. The ultimate stars of the show (with the exception of *Juggernaut)* are the acts of destruction per se.

We are optimistically reassured on a gut level that the authorities can limit the human toll of these disasters, while those same authorities' ideological notions of the priority of property over human life are reinforced. If a left-leaning disaster movie were ever produced, it would concentrate on people working collectively (a group hero) to cope with disaster and stress the calamity's costs to humanity.

Juggernaut, though not quite in this category, deserves to be set apart from the three other films under consideration because it focuses on the meaning of the impending disaster (a portending explosion aboard ship) for the mass of the passengers on board. Richard Lester's film is more than a vehicle for special effects and the overwhelming question of which pretty face will survive and which one will not. In this sharply edited and taut thriller, Richard Harris's bomb expert Fallon portrays an existential everyman, who faces death routinely in his day-to-day work. *Juggernaut's* intelligence and sense of humor places it several notches above the schlock of its more frenetic, hyped competition.

Like many cycles of Hollywood films made on the "imitate-it-while-it's-hot" principle, disaster films will undoubtedly outlive their appeal at the box office. Irwin Allen (producer of *Inferno* and the prototypical *Poseidon Adventure*) claims to have no less than nine smash-up epics in the works. Whatever images they seize upon, forthcoming disaster films will no doubt continue to offer acculturation to the "proper" social values of obedience to authority and obeisance to property. Until the form is exhausted, they will probably continue to appeal to a public that feels comfortable having these values reinforced.

Bibliography

A Selected Group of Books on Film and Society
Prepared by Garth Jowett

The following list contains forty selected books, all published since 1970, which examine various facets of the interrelationship between motion pictures and society. The emphasis is on studies which deal with film and American society, although a few books look at the problem in a more general way. Despite this list, all of which contribute to the literature, there is still a great deal of work to be done in this particular area.

Alloway, Lawrence. *Violent America: The Movies 1946-1964*. New York: Museum of Modern Art, 1971.

> An interesting examination of recurrent themes and motifs in American films between 1946 and 1964. The book is not really about violence, but about the relationship of films to society, and of films to other films.

Baldwin, James. *The Devil Finds Work*. New York: Dial Press, 1976.

> The noted author here turns his ever-perceptive eye to American films and offers his own personal visions of the interaction between these films and his own experiences. He reveals as much of himself as he does of the movies discussed. The book is a unique contribution to the "personal" literature of film analysis.

Bergman, Andrew. *We're in the Money: Depression America and Its Films*. New York: New York University Press, 1971.

> A useful examination of the American cinema of the Depression era, with an emphasis on the historical context, and suggestions as to why certain film genres emerged during this period.

Berton, Pierre. *Hollywood's Canada*. Toronto: McClelland & Stewart, 1975.

> A neglected (by the American press) examination of the way in which Hollywood films have "shaped" the image of Canada—not only for Americans, but for Canadians as well. The work is well written and carefully researched, and contributes a great deal to our understanding of the social and cultural importance of movies.

Braudy, Leo. *The World in a Frame: What We See in Films*. New York: Doubleday, 1977.

> An important book. Braudy examines the nature of film and explains in a clear, lucid manner the nature of the filmic experience. Braudy notes: "We need to look as closely and as openly as possible at what film in general has accomplished, instead of assuming that only occasional works of value could come from such a deficient and bastardized process."

Bogle, Donald. *Toms, Coons, Mulattoes, Mammies, & Bucks*. New York: Viking Press, 1973.

> Written by a former writer for *Ebony* magazine, this is one of the three important examinations of the treatment of blacks in American movies. Bogle's book suffers from a lack of documentation, but it is a sound contribution, with some particularly idiosyncratic views.

Cohn, Lawrence. *Movietone Presents the 20th Century*. New York: St. Martin's Press, 1976.

> This book covers the world in the period from 1919-63 as seen through the eyes of *20th Century Fox Movietone News*. A good combination of text and pictures, the book is a useful addition to the very sparse literature on the historically important newsreels.

Cripps, Thomas. *Slow Fade to Black: The Negro in American Film, 1900-1943*. New York: Oxford University Press, 1977.

> The best and most precise examination of the history of blacks in the American cinema. Based on several years of extensive research in public and private collections, this study adds enormously to our understanding of the problems that blacks faced when dealing with the Hollywood studio system, and how the film image of blacks coincided with the social philosophy prevalent at the time.

Facey, Paul W. *The Legion of Decency: A Sociological Analysis of the Emergence and Development of a Social Pressure Group.* New York: Arno Press, 1974.

The Legion of Decency played an important part in the history and development of the American motion picture industry, and yet there are almost no published materials dealing with its operation. This work is the best available source on the Legion's formation, ideology, operation, and ultimate effects.

Fadiman, William. *Hollywood Now.* London: Thames & Hudson, 1973.

Written by a former screenwriter with insider knowledge, this book analyzes with devastating frankness and wit the present situation in Hollywood. It concludes with a survey which reveals the problems and strengths, the hopes and illusions of Hollywood today.

Farber Stephen, *The Movie Rating Game.* Washington: Public Affairs Press, 1972.

This book examines an important, but neglected, aspect of the current American film scene—the Ratings of the Code and Rating Administration of the Motion Picture Association. Farber's account is a harrowing one and indicates the essential difficulties in trying to find a viable form of social control for the movies without violating the First Amendment.

Fell, John L. *Film and the Narrative Tradition.* Norman: University of Oklahoma Press, 1974.

A well-written examination of the early influences on the development of the motion picture. Fell suggests that the movies were offspring of the popular novels, graphic arts, comic books, music, and melodramas of the period.

Fielding, Raymond. *The American Newsreel, 1911-1967.* Norman: University of Oklahoma Press, 1972.

The newsreel was an important part of the popular American cinema in the pretelevision period. Fielding's well-researched book provides a great deal of useful information about how newsreels were made, and how they were affected by social pressures and the need for commercial expediency. Nevertheless, newsreels were a major source for pictorial news for millions of Americans for nearly fifty years.

Glucksmann, Andre. *Violence on the Screen*. London: British Film Institute, 1971.

> A short, but concise, examination of the different types of research into the possible effects of motion pictures on various audience groups.

Greenberg, Harvey R. *The Movies on Your Mind*. New York: E. P. Dutton, 1975.

> Greenberg is a psychoanalyst, and in this study he puts the movies "on the couch." The author goes after the "unconscious movie" hidden within the cinematic image, and he shows "the deeper conflicts and desires that resonate within our own psyches and keep our eyes glued to the screen."

Haskell, Molly. *From Reverence to Rape*. New York: Holt, Rinehart & Winston, 1973.

> A highly readable account of what the author calls "the betrayal" of women on the American screen. Examines the changing image of women in films and how the image has shifted from one of strength and independence to today's "raped and brutalized sex objects."

Higham, Charles. *Hollywood at Sunset: The Decline and Fall of the Most Colorful Empire Since Rome*. New York: Saturday Review Press, 1972.

> A behind-the-scenes examination of the problems that have beset Hollywood since 1946. Higham traces the economic decline due to television, and also puts much of the blame on the political problems associated with the "blacklist" and the fate of the "Hollywood Ten." While the book is a little sketchy in places, it is a most useful account of a vital period in American film history.

Jarvie, Ian. *Movies and Society*. New York: Basic Books, 1970.

> There are very few good books on the sociology of the cinema. Jarvie's work qualifies as one of the best, and it is also one of the few books to attempt a systematic analysis of those elements which go into the commerical motion picture. Sections include the Sociology of the Industry; the Sociology of the Audience; the Sociology of An Experience; and the Sociology of Evaluation. There is an added bonus of a detailed 137-page annotated bibliography.

Jowett, Garth. *Film: The Democratic Art.* Boston: Little, Brown, 1976.

A lengthy and detailed social history of moviegoing in America. This book is concerned with how film sought the acceptance of the American people and the obstacles which slowed the accommodation process, and what social, political, and cultural adjustments have been required for society to come to terms with this medium. The book concentrates on three aspects of the history of moviegoing: the changing composition of the film audience; individual and institutional reactions to film and how these changed with time; and the forces controlling the medium from within and without. This book contains data and tabular material not found in other motion picture histories.

Leab, Daniel J. *From Sambo to Superspade.* Boston: Houghton Mifflin, 1975.

One of the best accounts of the history of blacks on the American screen. Shows how the stereotype of the fawning, simple-minded and subhuman servant of the silent era has evolved into the impossibly virile heroes and heroines of today's "Blaxploitation" movies.

Lounsbury, Myron O. *The Origins of American Film Criticism, 1909-1939.* New York: Arno Press, 1973.

By carefully tracing the progressive development of the critical abilities of selected major film critics, Lounsbury is able to show how the motion picture assumed a major role on the American entertainment scene. The author clearly shows how the changing relationship between film and audience became a major factor in the development of a more sophisticated level of film criticism in America.

MacCann, Richard Dyer. *The People's Films.* New York: Hastings House, 1973.

An interesting and well-documented study of the documentary films produced by or for the U.S. government agencies. It is also a critical examination of factual films as educational and public relations media. MacCann's research covers the period from the turn of the century until the present and elucidates an unexplored topic.

MacCann, Richard Dyer, and Perry, Edward S. *The New Film Index.* New York: E. P. Dutton, 1975.

> The best and most useful of the new film bibliographies. This volume continues where the classic *The Film Index* edited by Harold Leonard left off in 1936. This new volume examines only magazine articles but is very comprehensive and quite easy to use. The annotations are particularly useful.

Maland, Charles. *American Visions: The Films of Chaplin, Ford, Capra, and Welles, 1936-1941.* New York: Arno Press, 1977.

> This detailed study examines the social and cultural significance of the films made by Chaplin, Ford, Capra, and Welles in the important period 1936-1941. The study focuses on the relationship between the director's films and his response to certain aspects of American culture. When taken as a whole, these films comprised a sensitive index to American history and a lasting record of imagination responding to a changing world.

Manvell, Roger. *Films and the Second World War.* Cranbury, N.J.: Barnes, 1974.

> The best of the recent spate of books on World War II movies. Manvell has taken the trouble to associate the films with social and cultural tensions, and his coverage includes films from both sides of the conflict. A very important addition to the literature.

Mason, John L. *The Identity Crisis Theme in American Feature Films, 1960-1969.* New York: Arno Press, 1977.

> A unique work in which the author interweaves psychology, communications theory, history, and film analysis to arrive at an intriguing examination of feature films of the 1960s. Of particular interest is the analysis of "wheeler" or motorcycle films. There is also a series of interviews which have never appeared before with notable directors and producers such as Roger Corman, Stanley Kramer, Larry Peerce, and Martin Ritt.

Mast, Gerald. *A Short History of the Movies.* Indianapolis: Bobbs-Merrill, 1976. 2nd ed.

> The best of the comprehensive histories of the cinema. While this book examines *world* film history, it is particularly strong on the American cinema and relates the development of the film as an art to social and cultural developments.

McClure, Arthur F., ed. *The Movies: An American Idiom*. Rutherford, N. J.: Fairleigh Dickinson University Press, 1971.

This book of readings in the social history of the American motion picture contains several important articles: "Censor the Movies!" by McClure, and "World War II and the American Film," by Lewis Jacobs are very useful historical summaries.

Paine, Jeffrey M. *The Simplification of American Life: Hollywood Films of the 1930s*. New York: Arno Press, 1977.

This study adds significantly to our understanding of an elusive subject—the American cinema of the 1930s. The author suggests that these films form a historical record of a "simplification of American life," as they contribute to the evolution of new values, new assumptions, and new modes of perception.

Richards, Jeffrey. *Visions of Yesterday*. London: Routledge & Kegan Paul, 1973.

A well-written study examining many facets of the interrelationship between film and society. There are sections on Nazi films, American "populist" films, and the films of British imperialism. Richards, a historian, opens new vistas of historical relevance for film scholars in this vital work.

Shain, Russell E. *An Analysis of Motion Pictures About War Released by the American Film Industry, 1939-1970*. New York: Arno Press, 1976.

The motion picture industry has long used the theme of war as a staple content form, but this subject has received little systematic examination. Shain's work is an important analysis of the war movie, and the role that such movie content plays in American society; it also clearly shows the changes required by the increasing importance of the international film market.

Sklar, Robert. *Movie-Made America*. New York: Random House, 1975.

This recent cultural history of the American cinema casts new light on the motion picture as a major factor in twentieth century cultural development. Sklar writes in a bold style, and the book is full of important insights which give the movies a new significance. In particular, Sklar's examination of the emergence of the movies out of their lower-class origins into a firm middle-class institution is a major contribution.

Smith, Julian. *Looking Away: Hollywood and Vietnam.* New York: Scribner's, 1975.

An imaginative examination of the political and cultural changes in the United States as reflected in the movies of the 1960s and 1970s which examined America's role in Europe and Asia. This book is a very personal account, but Smith writes very well and his views are interesting and provocative.

Stuart, Fredric. *The Effects of Television on the Motion Picture and Radio Industries.* New York: Arno Press, 1975.

The introduction of television had a devastating effect on the motion picture industry. Stuart's work is one of the few thorough analyses of the actual nature and extent of these effects. The author demonstrates that the introduction of television was the principal factor in bringing about the decline of the motion picture industry in the mid-1950s.

Toeplitz, Jerzy. *Hollywood and After: The Changing Face of American Cinema.* London: George Allen & Unwin, 1974.

Written by a former head of the Polish Film School, this book has its faults, particularly in translation ("Violence is . . . like cherry cake"—Rapp Brown, is the funniest example) but is nonetheless a useful and detailed examination of trends in Hollywood since the early 1960s. The European view on these changes is quite different from the American in many key places.

Tudor, Andrew. *Image and Influence: Studies in the Sociology of Film.* London: George, Allen & Unwin, 1974.

This is a useful examination of what sociologists know about the motion picture, and it suggests new lines of development. Looks at patterns of communication, movie communicators, audiences, patterns of culture, cinema and society, popular genres, and film movements.

Turan, Kenneth, and Zito, Stephen F. *Sinema.* New York: Praeger Publishers, Inc., 1974.

This semischolarly study of American pornographic films and the people who make them is an important contribution to our understanding of this genre. The tone is one of objectivity with no moralizing visible on the part of the authors. An extremely useful and interesting book.

Wenden, D. J. *The Birth of the Movies.* New York: E. P. Dutton, 1974.

Wenden examines the early history of the movies in a lively text. He seeks to explain how the cinema developed in the period and how it influenced social, economic, and political events in Europe and America.

Wood, Michael. *America at the Movies.* New York: Basic Books, 1975.

An idiosyncratic and nostalgic examination of some of the ways in which American society's fantasies have been worked out on the screen. While we all may not agree with Wood's interpretations, this is a very provocative and important book.

Wright, Will. *Sixguns and Society: A Structural Study of the Western.* Berkeley: University of California Press, 1975.

This study is something of a breakthrough, in that Wright has undertaken a full-scale study of one genre (the Western) using structural analysis. The tone is uncompromising and rigorous, but is unusually accessible for a structural analysis. Relying on Levi-Strauss's theories of myth, this is a provocative study and well worth the effort.